PRAY BETTER

LEARNING TO PRAY BIBLICALLY

Landon Coleman

Pray Better: Learning to Pray Biblically

ISBN 979-8-218-11450-3

Regular Pastor Publishing

Odessa, Texas

PRAISE FOR PRAY BETTER

"There is much I like about this book. It's biblical. It's practical. It's devotional. It's honest. It's pastoral. There's also something I really don't like about it, though — it's convicting. It reminds me that prayer should be in the DNA of believers. That's precisely why I — and, likely you — need to read it."

Chuck Lawless
Vice President for Graduate Studies, SEBTS
Global Theological Education Consultant, IMB

Acknowledgements

To the Wednesday night prayer warriors at North Benson Baptist Church, First Baptist Church Kingfisher, and Immanuel Baptist Church... Thank you for praying with me for our churches. Thank you for the privilege of studying Bible prayers with you. Thank you for your invaluable questions and insights. As iron sharpens iron, so you have sharpened me (Proverbs 27:17).

CONTENTS

INTRODUCTION

HELLO. MY NAME IS LANDON. I'M A PASTOR. AND I STRUGgle with prayer. There. I said it. I think prayer is hard. Maybe it's just me, or maybe it's my personality, but I think prayer is by far the hardest spiritual discipline. Set me in a room with a Bible and a stack of books, and I can study all day long. Tell me to journal about my spiritual experience, and I can fill a Moleskine notebook with the best of them. Hand me a guitar and a chord sheet, and I can strum and sing for hours. But sit me down and ask me to pray for twenty minutes? Odds are I'll be asleep in five.

I don't know why I struggle so much with prayer. I grew up in a Christian home. I was raised in a fantastic church. I know all about the importance of prayer. I studied under great men of prayer during my time in seminary. I've listened to sermons about prayer and read books about prayer. But still I struggle with prayer. Maybe it has something to do with the fact that I am incredibly task-oriented and feel the constant need to get something done. Maybe it has something to do with the fact that I have the attention span of a goldfish. Or, maybe I have something in common with the disciples who struggled to pray with Jesus in Gethsemane (Mat-

9

thew 26:36-46). Who knows? Maybe it's just me. Maybe I'm the only one who thinks prayer is hard.

Or maybe I'm not the only one. Honestly, I don't think I'm the only one who struggles with prayer, nor do I think I'm the only pastor who struggles with prayer. I've read different surveys about how much time people spend in prayer each day. I've even done surveys of my own. My first thought when I read these surveys is that my prayer life is embarrassingly pathetic. My second thought is that people lie about their prayer life. Seriously, who wants to admit they haven't prayed since last Thursday? I don't want to admit that, and I don't think most Christians do either.

I know other people are just as busy as I am. I think other people have a tendency to daydream or doze off in the middle of a prayer. I think other people struggle with not knowing what to pray and unintentionally repeating the same thing over and over. I think other people struggle with how much time they ought to spend in prayer and how often they ought to set aside time to pray. I think other pastors struggle with public prayer, wanting their corporate prayers to be long enough that people think the pastor knows what he's doing, but short enough that people don't think we're trying to catch up from a week without prayer.

So for all those reasons, I believe prayer is hard. And while I'm being honest, I'd also like to say that I believe prayer is perplexing. Quite frankly, there are some things about prayer that just don't make sense. For example, I believe the God of the Bible is totally sovereign (see Romans 9) and fully omniscient (see Psalm 139). Theologically, I struggle to fit prayer into that mix. And if you think you have a pithy phrase that will untie that theological knot, I don't want hear it because I can almost guarantee the theology undergirding your pithiness is suspect.

For me this is a major theological issue. If God does whatever he wants to do whenever he wants to do it (I believe that he does), and if God knows the future from the beginning and everything in between (I believe that he does), what real significance can I attach to my puny prayers? Flowing out of this theological issue is a common sense issue worth mentioning. If I am small and know virtually nothing (I believe this is true), and if God is big and knows literally everything (I believe this is true), why in the world would I want to do so much talking?

On top of all that, there are a few things that annoy me about prayer. One is the fact that in my 31 years of church life almost every prayer list I've ever seen is nothing more than a catalogue of sick people, with a few missionaries tacked on to the end. I've pastored three churches. As a pastor, I've always made an effort to keep the official prayer list from becoming a directory of the infirm. And I always end up feeling guilty for being the prayer list cur- mudgeon and constantly taking people off the sick list.

A related frustration is the tendency in Christian circles to suggest that more people praying equals more powerful prayer. In other words, I've heard sincere Christians suggest that if we could just get a few more people praying, then maybe God would listen to us and do what we want him to do. Surely this is not a biblical view of God, is it? Surely God isn't waiting for us to rally 10 more prayer warriors to our cause? Surely God isn't waiting for our email prayer chain to get forwarded to 100 more people? Surely prayer isn't like a civic petition that requires a minimum number of signatures to be considered valid?

So for all these reasons, I think prayer is hard, perplexing, and at times annoying.

Then I sit down to read the Bible. After all, I think this is a much more pleasant spiritual discipline. That is, until I get to the prayers. I read about godly men and women in the Old Testament who prayed. People like Abraham and Moses and Hannah and Hezekiah. I read their prayers, I sense their passion, and I'm ashamed.

Then it gets worse. I read about Jesus, God in human flesh, the Creator of all things, going off by himself to pray (Matthew 14:23, Luke 5:16). I read that sometimes Jesus, the Healer of the sick, the Feeder of thousands, the Master of demons, would pray all night (Luke 6:12). I hear Jesus, Truth incarnate, telling me that I ought to pray persistently without giving up (Luke 18:1). Suddenly my confusion about prayer seems irrelevant, my annoyance with prayer seems evil, and I feel like I ought to hide under a rock.

I need to pray more. I need to pray better. I need to learn from the godly men and women whose prayers are recorded in the Bible. I need to learn from Jesus himself about what and when and how often to pray. This book is a collection of some of the things I have learned studying the prayers of the Bible. There are plenty of Bible passages that teach about prayer, and those passages are important. This book focuses on twenty of the actual prayers of the Bible. Many good prayers were left out, and no attempt was made to balance Old Testament and New Testament prayers. A comprehensive and balanced treatment is not my goal. My personal hope in studying these passages is that I would learn how to pray. My hope in writing this book is that you would learn how to pray.

CHAPTER 1

ABRAHAM PRAYS FOR SODOM

Shall not the Judge of all the earth do what is just? (Genesis 18:25)

IN GENESIS 12 YAHWEH INTRODUCED HIMSELF TO ABRAM. Before this introduction, Abram and his family worshipped statues of wood and stone (Joshua 24:2). After this introduction, Abram became a follower of Yahweh. Following Yahweh meant Abram had to leave his family and home to travel to an unknown place. Remarkably, Abram and his wife Sarai left family and home, trusting in Yahweh's promises of land, offspring, and blessing (Genesis 12:1-10).

After a brief sojourn in Egypt (Genesis 12:10-20), Abram and his wife Sarai had a pivotal conversation with their relative Lot. Lot had been traveling with Abram and Sarai for some time (Genesis 12:4). However, because of the blessing of Yahweh, the land could not support the families and flocks of both men (Genesis 13:5-7). Thus, the pivotal decision was made. Abram and Lot would part ways. Lot took his family and flocks toward the Jordan Valley, and Abram took his family and flocks toward the land of Canaan (Genesis 13:8-12). After this separation Yahweh again appeared to Abram and once again promised land, offspring, and blessing (Genesis 13:14-18).

At this point the Bible mentions an important detail. Genesis 13:12-13 explains, "Abram settled in the land of Canaan, while Lot settled among the cities of the valley and moved his tent as far as Sodom. Now the men of Sodom were wicked, great sinners against the LORD." This is not the last we hear of Lot, nor is it the last we hear of Sodom.

In Genesis 14 we read of disaster falling on the people of Sodom. A group of local kings made an alliance and attacked Sodom (Genesis 14:1-12). When Sodom fell to this alliance of kings, Lot and his family were taken as plunder (Genesis 14:12). The final half of Genesis 14 tells of a heroic rescue mission undertaken by Abram (Genesis 14:13-24). In light of the infamous wickedness of Sodom, and in light of the experience of being kidnapped by an invading army, one might expect Lot to relocate his family to a safer community. Unfortunately, this is not the last we hear of Lot or Sodom.

Genesis 15 details yet another conversation between Yahweh and Abram. This time Yahweh appeared to Abram in a vision and promised protection and offspring (Genesis 15:1-5). In response to these promises, the elderly Abram believed Yahweh, and his faith was credited to him as righteousness (Genesis 15:6). While the childless Abram believed God would make good on his promises, he began to wonder *how* God would make good on his promises. In light of his age and Sarai's barrenness, this elderly couple wondered if God might make good on his promises through Hagar, Sarai's servant. After all, the promises of God had centered on Abram, not Sarai. Perhaps this was *how* God planned on making good on his promises. Genesis 16 describes Abram and Sarai foolishly acting on the old maxim, "God helps those who help themselves." Abram slept with Hagar. Hagar became pregnant, and she gave birth to a son named Ishmael (Genesis 16:1-16).

On the heels of this affair, Yahweh once again appeared to Abram. In this conversation, just one year before Abram's one-hundredth birthday, Yahweh insisted that barren Sarai would conceive and give birth to a son named Isaac (Genesis 17:15-21). As a sign that Abram believed this covenant promise, all the males in Abram's family were to be circumcised (Genesis 17:1-14). As if that weren't enough, Yahweh also asked Abram to change his name from Abram (father of many) to Abraham (father of a multitude). Once again, Abram did what Yahweh asked of him (Genesis 17:22-27). He circumcised himself and his family, which resulted in physical pain. He also changed his name to Abraham, which certainly resulted in mockery and emotional pain.

Sometime later, with Yahweh's promises still unfulfilled, Yahweh appeared to Abram by the oak trees of Mamre (Genesis 18:1). The same old promises were once again made to Abram and Sarai, this time with a one-year time-table (Genesis 18:9-15). On the heels of this conversation, the author of Genesis records a fascinating conversation between Abram and Yahweh. Take a few minutes to read Genesis 18:16-33.

The story that follows this conversation details the destruction of Sodom and Gomorrah. It is a story that illustrates God's righteous anger towards sin, a theme that is absent from many pulpits and churches. The story also highlights the absence of even ten righteous people in these wicked cities. Again, the theme of human depravity is one that is often neglected in many pulpits and churches. While other important lessons can be gleaned from the story, our focus is Abraham's prayer of intercession for the cities of Sodom and Gomorrah. This prayer was surely based on the fact that Abraham knew Lot was dwelling in the city of Sodom (Genesis 19:1). When Abraham learned what Yahweh had planned for the city in which his family lived, Abraham responded with prayer.

One important thing to note is the fact that Abraham's prayer came in the context of relationship, faith, and obedience. Abraham knew Yahweh. Abraham believed the promises of Yahweh even though they had not yet been fulfilled. Abraham understood the importance of obedience. He left home and family. He circumcised his family. He changed his name. Abraham knew Yahweh as "the Judge of all the earth," and he was convinced that Yahweh would ultimately do the right thing (Genesis 18:25). Genesis 19 is not the story of a man coming to God and desperately begging for a favor from a stranger. Genesis 19 is the story of a man pleading with a God he knew, trusted, and obeyed.

Also important is the humility Abraham exhibited in this prayer. In verse 27 Abraham acknowledges that Yahweh does not have to listen, and he acknowledges his human frailty. In verses 30 and 32 Abraham prefaces his questions with a request that Yahweh not be angry. Abraham wasn't concerned that Yahweh would be angry with the specific question. Abraham was concerned that Yahweh would be angry with the act of questioning. In other words, Abraham understood that the very act of talking to Yahweh was a privilege, not a right. This idea is reinforced in verse 33 where the author of Genesis tells us that Yahweh "went his way, when he had finished speaking to Abraham." What a shocking verse! Most people would expect the verse to say God went his way when Abraham was finished talking. Most people operate under the assumption that God is obligated to listen to our prayers. Genesis 18:33 reminds us that God can leave any conversation whenever he pleases.

A final noteworthy aspect of this prayer is Abraham's persistence. Six times Abraham asked the same question of Yahweh. Only the number of righteous people in question changed. Certainly this persistence was rooted in Abraham's love for Lot, but it also reveals something that Abraham knew to be true of Yahweh. Abraham knew he had to come before Yahweh in humility, and he knew the act of conversation was itself a privilege. But Abraham also knew the character of Yahweh. Abraham knew the God who had saved him from idolatry was a God of mercy. Abraham knew the God who had remained faithful to his promises was a God of grace. So Abraham persisted in prayer for Lot and Sodom.

May our prayers be persistent. May our prayers be humble. May our prayers flow out of a relationship with God that is marked by faith and obedience.

LEARNING TO PRAY

Tom and Karen live in a small town in western Oklahoma. They are well respected in the community and active members of a local church. Despite the distance between New York City and western Oklahoma, Tom and Karen were rocked by the terrorist attacks of September 11, 2001. Eight months later, when their son Sam graduated high school and joined the Army, Tom and Karen were conflicted. On the one hand, they considered themselves patriotic, so having a son serve in the military made them proud. On the other hand, their only child was headed into combat with no guarantee of safe return.

Sam deployed three times. During these deployments Tom and Karen faithfully prayed for their son. They sent a weekly email to their closest family and friends reminding them to pray for Sam. They also mentioned Sam every Wednesday at their church prayer meeting. Three times Sam deployed into combat. Three times Sam returned home. Tom and Karen personally experienced the power of prayer.

Strangely enough, a decade later Tom is struggling. He's the first to admit that most of his prayers for Sam were answered. Sam moved on from the Army to a great job in Oklahoma. He married his high school sweetheart, and they have two sons. And yet Tom struggles. His struggle has nothing to do with prayers that were answered. His struggle has everything to do with prayers that were not answered. Tom wonders about the military families who were not as fortunate as his. Tom thinks about his friend Joe. Because of a roadside bomb, Joe's son came back from Iraq with only one leg. Tom thinks about Bill. Because of a Taliban ambush, Bill's son never came home from Afghanistan.

It may seem strange, but Tom feels guilty that his son returned home safely while others did not. Tom knows his friends prayed for their sons. Should they have prayed more? Should they have prayed better? Tom wonders why God answered his prayers but not the prayers of his friends.

He begins to understand when he turns to Genesis 18 and reads about Abraham's prayer for Sodom. First, Tom is encouraged by Abraham's persistence. Looking back, he knows the emails and prayer meetings were not in vain. At the same time, Tom is convicted by Abraham's humility. Even though he had an incredibly intimate relationship with God, Abraham approached God with humility. He also trusted God to do what was right. In the end, God did not spare Sodom and Gomorrah as Abraham hoped, but God did show grace even in the midst of unanswered prayer. This gives Tom a measure of peace. He begins to realize that prayer is less about manipulating God to accept your suggestions and more about a relationship based on faith. Tom begins to pray with humility, trusting God to do right, and looking for grace in the midst of unanswered prayer.

QUESTIONS FOR DISCUSSION

1. Have you been guilty of coming to God as a stranger asking for favors? If so, what do you need to do to grow in genuine relationship with God?

2. Are you expecting God to answer your prayers without first following God in obedience?

3. How are humility and persistence balanced in your
    prayer life?

CHAPTER 2

MOSES PRAYS FOR
ISRAEL

*But now, if you will forgive their sin – but if not,
please blot me out of your book that you have
written. (Exodus 32:32)*

GOD MADE SEVERAL COVENANT PROMISES TO ABRAHAM
(Genesis 12:1-3, 15:1-19, 17:1-14). These covenant promises
were first passed to Abraham's son Isaac (not Ishmael),
then to Isaac's son Jacob (not Esau). In time Jacob
had twelve sons: Reuben, Simeon, Levi, Judah, Dan,
Naphtali, Gad, Asher, Issachar, Zebulun, Joseph, and
Benjamin. Thus Abraham's great-grandsons became the
twelve tribes of Israel. The covenant promises God made
to Abraham decades earlier were actually beginning
to come true. The family of a once childless man was
beginning to grow. At this point in the story, his family

reunions didn't yet measure up to the number of stars in the sky, but Abraham's family was several dozen strong.

Then a famine hit the land of Abraham's great-grand-sons. Through a remarkable series of events, Abraham's great-grandson Joseph ended up in Egypt (Genesis 37-50). Despite the evil intentions of Joseph's brothers, God had a plan to use the situation for their good and his glory (Genesis 50:20). Abraham's family survived the famine by taking refuge in Egypt. They had left the land God promised them, but they continued to hope in the promises of God. When Joseph was dying, he told his brothers, "God will visit you and bring you up out of this land to the land that he swore to Abraham, to Isaac, and to Jacob." (Genesis 50:24)

This prophetic word certainly brought hope to Abraham's descendants, hope that one day they might return to the land God had promised to Abraham. What they didn't know at the time is that in spite of all of Joseph's power and influence in Egypt, a new Pharaoh was on the horizon. This new Pharaoh did not care about Joseph or his family (Exodus 1:8-10). Consequently, while Abraham's family continued to grow in numbers, these Hebrew babies were born as slaves in Egypt. The story of rescue that follows is nothing short of spectacular. God not only preserved the life of Moses (Exodus 2:1-10), he also used Moses to bring crushing disaster on Pharaoh (Exodus 3-12). The result of this disaster was the exodus of Abraham's family from Egypt (Exodus 13-15).

After redeeming his people, God brought them to Mt. Sinai where he intended to give Moses the Law so that he could in turn give the Law to Israel. Moses and his faithful assistant Joshua ventured up the mountain to meet with God. Meanwhile, Moses' brother Aaron was left in charge of the people. Tragically, and ironically, while Moses was receiving the Ten Commandments on Mt. Sinai, Aaron and the people were breaking the Ten Commandments at the foot of Mt. Sinai (Exodus 32:1-10). This was a catastrophic turn of events. These people sincerely believed they were worshipping "the LORD," but they had created an idol in the image of a cow. In response to God's righteous anger, Moses prayed on behalf of the people. Take a moment to read Moses' intercessory prayer in Exodus 32:11-14.

The first words out of Moses' mouth were a question. He asked God why he would want to destroy what he had redeemed with such magnificent power and might (Exodus 32:11). Second, Moses prayed that God would not give the Egyptians reason to blaspheme the name of the LORD (Exodus 32:12). Finally, Moses prayed that God would remember his covenant promises to Abraham, Isaac, and Jacob. After praying this prayer, Moses went down to check on Aaron and the people.

Unfortunately, things below were every bit as depraved as God had told Moses. When Moses saw the people breaking God's law, Moses broke the tablets of stone containing the Ten Commandments (Exodus 32:19).

Then he smashed Aaron's golden calf into dust and made the people drink their idol (Exodus 32:20). A few verses later we read about Moses' plan to once again pray to the LORD on behalf of the sinful people. Again, take a moment to read Moses' second intercessory prayer in Exodus 32:30-35.

This is a remarkable prayer, and it sheds light on the idea that Moses was the most meek, humble man on earth (Numbers 12:3). Moses actually prayed for the people who previously murmured against him (something Jesus talked about in Matthew 5:44). And amazingly Moses asked God to blot his name out of the book instead of the names of these idol worshipping rebels. Moses was so consumed with a passion for God's glory (see his previous prayer, Exodus 32:11-14), he offered to take the fall for Israel. The only problem with Moses' suggestion here is Moses himself. Although not guilty of worshipping the golden calf, Moses was a sinner. And as a sinner, Moses was not fit to take anyone's place in judgment. Remember, God told Moses, "Whoever has sinned against me, I will blot out of my book." (Exodus 32:33)

As we think about prayer in our lives, this scenario leads us to the first of several truths we must understand. Moses' willingness to stand in the place of sinful Israel clearly points us to Jesus who stood in the place of sinful humans. The Bible shows how Jesus became sin for us and died for our rebellion (2 Corinthians 5:21, Galatians 3:13-14, 1 Peter 2:24-25). And whether we want to admit it or not, our rebellion is no worse than Israel's. Praise God! What Moses offered to do in Exodus 32, Jesus actually did on the cross! When we pray "in Jesus' name," we're not just adding the finishing touches to an otherwise incomplete prayer. Rather we are acknowledging that our ability to speak to the Father is a result of the earth-shattering truth that Jesus was blotted out in our place.

Another truth we need to take away from Exodus 32 is the idea that while God is certainly gracious and forgiving, sometimes the consequences of our sin remain. In this story we see God's grace on several levels. Even though Aaron acted as the ringleader of this idolatrous affair, he was allowed to serve as the first High Priest of Israel. Also, God did listen to Moses' prayer and stayed his hand of judgment against Israel as a whole. These examples remind us that when we pray, we pray to a God who is gracious and forgiving and patient and slow to anger.

However, there were serious consequences for Israel's sin. The Bible details that the sons of Levi rallied to Moses' side and killed 3,000 of their kinsman who had bowed to the golden calf (Exodus 32:25-29). The Bible also explains that even after Moses prayed a second time, the LORD sent a plague because of the golden calf Aaron had made (Exodus 32:35). So was God gracious in response to Moses' prayers? Absolutely, God was gracious. But there were consequences. And as we pray to the God of grace, we must remember that his forgiveness does not always remove the consequences of our sin.

One last truth to take away from this passage is one that must constantly undergird every aspect of our prayer lives. In this story we are reminded that God ordains the ends as well as the means. In other words, in his infinite and eternal wisdom, God had planned to extend mercy and grace to these undeserving people. Additionally, in his infinite and eternal wisdom, God has planned to move Moses to prayer and to hear Moses' prayer.

Talking about this very incident, Psalm 106:23 notes, "Therefore [God] said he would destroy them – had not Moses, his chosen one, stood in the breach before him, to turn away his wrath from destroying them." Think about that. God would have destroyed the people if Moses, God's chosen one, had not stood in the gap to pray for Israel. Moses' prayer was not a last minute plan-B that unexpectedly moved the LORD to compassion. Rather, Moses was God's "chosen one" from eternity past to intercede for the people. Does that mean God was going to extend grace and mercy regardless of whether or not Moses prayed? Not according to Psalm 106:23 which explains God would have destroyed the people if Moses had not prayed. Yes God ordained the end, grace and mercy for Israel. But he also ordained the means, the prayer of Moses. And the eternal plans of God did not make Moses' prayer less critical. He would have destroyed the people had not Moses prayed on their behalf. Prayer matters.

LEARNING TO PRAY

Cindy and Jim met in college. At first it seemed like a match made in heaven. They met at a college Bible study, they shared a passion for world missions, they both wanted a large family, and they even enjoyed the same movies. No one was surprised when Jim proposed six months into their relationship. One week after Cindy graduated college the happy couple was on their honeymoon.

Then life hit like a hurricane. Cindy got pregnant on the honeymoon. Jim only needed one more semester to graduate, but he decided to put college on hold. The newlyweds needed money and insurance, which meant Jim needed a job. Without a degree he had to settle for the night shift. Jim said it was only temporary. One day he would finish college. One day they would settle into a normal routine. But for now they needed income and insurance, so Jim took the night job.

From there everything snowballed into disaster. Jim was usually too tired to go to church after working all night. Cindy hated going to church without Jim. Even worse, Cindy was terribly lonely with Jim working nights and sleeping during the day. While they were dating they did everything together. Now they were lucky to talk five minutes a day. After their daughter was born, things got worse. Now Cindy was lonely and left with the task of taking care of a baby by herself.

Cindy never planned on having an affair, but that's what happened. The Facebook message from an old friend seemed so innocent. Unfortunately Cindy didn't realize how loneliness and bitterness set her up for temptation. Soon she found herself doing something she never thought she would do. When Jim found out, he left immediately. Cindy was broken. Her repentance was genuine. But for Jim it was too little too late.

In the months following the divorce Cindy prayed more than she had ever prayed in her life. She prayed that God would forgive her, but she didn't feel forgiven. Other than praying for forgiveness, Cindy mostly prayed about the consequences of her sin. She prayed that God would fix what she destroyed. She prayed that God would take away the pain and the hurt. She prayed that God would remove her regret and embarrassment. Nevertheless, after months of prayer, Jim moved on to a new relationship. Cindy began to accept the reality that things would never go back to normal.

This realization drove Cindy to look for answers in the Bible. In Exodus 32 she found a God of grace and forgiveness. She found assurance that even her sin could be covered by the blood of Christ. Instead of repeatedly asking for forgiveness that didn't seem real, Cindy began thanking God for forgiveness that was purchased by Jesus. These verses also helped Cindy accept the fact that forgiveness does not remove all consequences. Instead of asking God to remove the consequences of her sin,

Cindy began asking God to do a good work in her life, in her daughter's life, and even in Jim's life.

Questions for Discussion

1. Are you trying to pray without first entering into a relationship with Jesus? If so, will you repent of your sin and trust Jesus now?

2. In your prayers, are you obsessing on the consequences of your sin? These may be consequences that God is not going to remove even though your sin is forgiven.

3. How does your belief in God's sovereignty impact your prayer life? Do you pray like your prayers really matter?

CHAPTER 3

MOSES PRAYS ABOUT
THE PROMISED LAND

*Please let me go over and see the good land be-
yond the Jordan. (Deuteronomy 3:25)*

MOSES LIVED AN EXTRAORDINARY LIFE. FROM THE TIME
he was born until the time God buried him, Moses saw
and experienced the amazing and the miraculous. His
parents were Hebrew slaves in Egypt, and his birth
coincided with Pharaoh's decree that all male Hebrew
babies should bc killed (Exodus 1:8-2:10). By the grace
of God, Moses' life was spared, and in the greatest of
ironies Moses was actually raised as Pharaoh's grandson
(Exodus 2:9-10).

At this point, Hollywood has not been able to resist
speculating about the drama that was certainly involved
in Moses' upbringing. The Bible is more restrained in

providing details, and we simply read, "One day, when Moses had grown up, he went out to his people and looked on their burdens, and he saw an Egyptian beating a Hebrew, one of his people." (Exodus 2:11) In response to this violence, Moses murdered the Egyptian and buried him in the sand (Exodus 2:12). Again, Hollywood speculates about the drama and intrigue involved in this retaliatory act. And again, the Bible is more restrained in simply telling us that Moses ran away into the wilderness as soon as he realized that his crime was public knowledge (Exodus 2:15).

In the wilderness of Midian, Moses took up shepherding and took a wife (Exodus 2:16-22). Just when Moses thought life was settling into a nice routine, God turned Moses' life upside down. God appeared to Moses in the bush that burned without being consumed, and he sent Moses back to Egypt to confront the new Pharaoh (Exodus 3:1-4:31). With Aaron at his side, Moses returned to Egypt. Through Moses, God sent ten devastating plagues against Pharaoh and his people (Exodus 7:1-12:32). The last plague was absolutely crushing as the LORD struck down firstborns throughout Egypt. Pharaoh tapped out, and the exodus ensued (Exodus 12:22-42).

Up to the exodus, Moses' life had been a giant adventure to say the least. After the exodus, the adventure continued. Moses walked through the Red Sea after God split the water in two (Exodus 14). Moses and the people ate bread from heaven (Exodus 16). Moses and the people drank water from a rock (Exodus 17). Moses watched Joshua lead Israel in battle (Exodus 17). Moses even met God face-to-face and received the Ten Commandments on Mt. Sinai (Exodus 19-20). To balance out these mostly positive adventures, Moses also experienced his fair share of heartbreak. Moses witnessed Israel worship a golden calf (Exodus 32). Moses faced a coup from his own siblings (Numbers 12). Moses received the pessimistic and faithless report of the spies (Numbers 13). Moses watched the earth swallow Korah and his family (Numbers 16). Through all of these adventures, Moses found himself wandering in the wilderness with a bunch of ungrateful, stiff-necked, malcontents. Moses longed for the day he would finally set foot in the Promised Land.

Then, after decades in the wilderness, we read about a disastrous chapter in Moses' life. In Numbers 20 we learn that Moses' sister Miriam and brother Aaron both died a short time before the people would enter the Promised Land. Other than Joshua and Caleb, these funerals basically left Moses as the last of the exodus generation. In between these funerals, we read about the nadir of Moses' life.

In Numbers 20, the people quarreled with Moses because once again they needed water for their families and flocks. Humanly speaking, this was a reasonable concern. Water is a necessity, not a luxury. Spiritually speaking, the people should have learned to trust God to provide anything and everything they needed. When this complaint came to Moses, he did what he should have done as the leader of Israel. He went to the LORD for help. God responded to Moses' plea for help with these very specific, very clear directions: "Take the staff, and assemble the congregation, you and Aaron your brother, and tell the rock before their eyes to yield its water." (Numbers 20:8)

At this point it is worth remembering that a similar scenario played out earlier in Exodus 17:1-7. At Rephidim the people had quarreled with Moses about a lack of water, Moses had asked God for help, and God had responded with these very specific, very clear directions: "Take in your hand the staff with which you struck the Nile, and go. Behold, I will stand before you there on the rock at Horeb, and you shall strike the rock, and water shall come out of it." (Exodus 17:6)

Notice that these directions are slightly different than those Moses received in Numbers 20. In Exodus 17 God told Moses he himself would stand before Moses on the rock as Moses struck the rock with his staff. The New Testament confirms that Christ was the rock Moses struck (1 Corinthians 10:1-5). The image should be obvious. God himself is struck so his people can receive the provision they need. This scene with Moses striking the rock looked back to the gospel promises of Genesis 3:15. It also looked forward to the gospel fulfillment of John 3:16.

But in Numbers 20, God chose not to repeat this scene. In Numbers 20 God clearly told Moses to take his staff, gather the people, and *tell* the rock to bring forth water. Moses did take the staff. Moses did gather the people. But instead of telling the rock to bring forth water, Moses hit the rock with his staff. When nothing happened, he did it again. After the second blow, water came out of the rock and the people were refreshed.

God was not amused, and Numbers 20:12 records God's words to Moses: "Because you did not believe in me, to uphold me as holy in the eyes of the people of Israel, therefore you shall not bring this assembly into the land that I have given them." This is shocking! After all that Moses has experienced as God's chosen leader of Israel, after all the highs and all the lows, Moses did not believe God or uphold God as holy in the eyes of the people. The consequence for Moses was crushing. Moses would not be allowed to enter the Promised Land with the people. Instead, he would die in the wilderness just like the rest of the generation who refused to fight decades earlier.

This was a devastating blow for Moses, and in the face of great disappointment, Moses prayed. Deuteronomy 3:23-25 contains the following prayer, one that oozes with heartache: "And I pleaded with the LORD at that time, saying, 'O Lord GOD, you have only begun to show your servant your greatness and your mighty hand. For what god is there in heaven or on earth who can do such works and mighty acts as yours? Please let me go over and see the good land beyond the Jordan, that good hill country and Lebanon.'"

First, notice that Moses was pleading with the LORD. This was no casual rehearsing of prayer requests. This was urgent, serious, heartfelt prayer. Second, notice that Moses acknowledges the greatness and the power and the uniqueness of God. His prayer was grounded on solid theology. Third, notice that God heard Moses' prayer and provided an answer. Deuteronomy 3:26-28 demonstrates this: "But the LORD was angry with me because of you and would not listen to me. And the LORD said to me, 'Enough from you; do not speak to me of this matter again. Go up to the top of Pisgah and lift up your eyes westward and northward and southward and eastward, and look at it with your eyes, for you shall not go over this Jordan. But charge Joshua, and encourage and strengthen him, for he shall go over at the head of this people, and he shall put them in possession of the land that you shall see.' So we remained in the valley opposite Beth-peor."

Clearly this was not the answer Moses was hoping for. Not only did God say "no," but he also told Moses he was not to ask about this again. Ever. If there was a passage in the Bible that clearly reminds us that our prayers are not magic or automatic, that God does not always heed our advice, that God sometimes says no, this is that passage.

But the fact that God sometimes says "no" is not the only lesson we need to learn about prayer. We also need to understand that even when God says "no" he is gracious to his people. Although Moses had done nothing to merit God's grace, God told Moses he would be allowed to see the Promised Land (Deuteronomy 3:27). And as an act of delayed grace, Moses was eventually allowed to set foot in the Promised Land. Centuries later, when Jesus revealed his glory to three of his disciples, Moses and Elijah were sent to stand with Jesus (Matthew 17:1-8). Luke even tells us that Jesus, Moses, and Elijah talked about the crucifixion (Luke 9:30). Not only did Moses have the privilege of speaking with Jesus about the most important event in human history. He also had the privilege of standing in the Promised Land for the first time. Even though the answer to Moses' prayer was "no," God was gracious to Moses.

It's also worth noting that after God told Moses "no," he in turn asked Moses to do something that was certainly difficult. God asked Moses to charge Joshua, encourage Joshua, and strengthen Joshua for the task of leading Israel into the Promised Land (Deuteronomy 3:28-29). Basically, God asked Moses to equip Joshua to do the job Moses himself wanted to do. This was undoubtedly a challenge. Moses heard God say "no." Moses heard God tell him to drop the issue, forever. Moses heard God tell him to do something that was just about the opposite of what he wanted to do.

And in spite of all that bad news, Moses obeyed. He did not complain. He did not argue. He did not walk away from God. He simply obeyed. Deuteronomy 3:29 is not providing an incidental detail when it describes, "So we remained in the valley opposite Beth-peor." Moses was close enough to see the Promised Land. He had walked many thousands of miles in his life, and now he was only a few miles away from the Promised Land. All he had to do was walk down the mountain and cross the Jordan. I've often wondered if Moses contemplated making a mad dash for the Jordan. What we know is that Moses obeyed. He stayed put and did what God called him to do. The rest of Deuteronomy is the story of Moses commissioning the people one last time, encouraging them to follow God and Joshua. Where Moses failed in Numbers 20 is where he passed in Deuteronomy 3.

God doesn't always answer our prayers the way we want him to. In fact, sometimes God tells us, "No, and don't ask anymore." And sometimes God asks us to do the very thing we least want to do. However, Deuteronomy 3 reminds us that even when the answer is "no," God is gracious. May our prayers always be submissive to his will, and may our obedience always be swift and complete.

LEARNING TO PRAY

John had big dreams in college. His advisor assured him a degree in computer science would lead to a big payday down the road. John excelled in his coursework and had no trouble finding a job upon graduation. However, twenty years later John was stuck. It was a perfect storm really. First, the market was flooded with computer science grads who apparently received the same advice John received. Then the economy tanked, and jobs became scarce. On the one hand John was grateful to have a job. He knew plenty of people who would gladly take his place for a paycheck. On the other hand, John was severely disappointed with his lot in life. Things just didn't work out like he had dreamed they would. The promotion and the corner office and the big payday never materialized.

Even though he was a follower of Jesus, John didn't really know how to deal with his frustrations. But he knew he was supposed to bring all of his anxieties to God in prayer. So that's what he did. John spent an inordinate amount of time complaining to God about his job. He was always careful to throw in an obligatory "thank you" for the job he had. But he quickly moved on to reminding God why he wanted a different job, a better job. He regularly acknowledged that other people had it far worse than he did. After all, there were starving children in China. But then he moved on to beg for a promotion or a raise or a transfer or anything.

In his honest moments, John would admit that his job wasn't all bad. He worked with some great people, and twenty years with the same group of people had resulted in solid relationships. He considered several of his coworkers genuine friends, and he had even led two coworkers to become followers of Christ. Another bright spot was the office Bible study. After inviting everyone to church multiple times, several people asked John to start an office Bible study during lunch on Wednesdays. This had been a great opportunity for John to share his faith with some of his coworkers who refused to come to church on Sunday. Although no one called him the office chaplain, that's basically what John had become over the last twenty years. People knew they could come to John to ask Bible questions, to get advice, or even to request prayer.

One week John studied Deuteronomy 3 for the Wednesday office Bible study. As he read Moses' prayer he realized his own prayers needed to change. He had begged for a better job for twenty years. That job was nowhere in sight. Maybe God's answer was no. Maybe God had something important for John to do at his dead end job. Maybe his calling wasn't the corner office or the big payday. Maybe God wanted function as the office chaplain for another twenty years. Maybe God wanted him to disciple the new guy, Richard. Maybe God wanted him to stay put at his dead end job until he retired. From that day forward, John's prayers changed. John stopped complaining to God. John stopped reminding God of what he wanted so badly. Instead, John prayed that God would help him see what he needed to do in his office, and John prayed for the strength to do what God called him to do.

QUESTIONS FOR DISCUSSION

1. Are you desperately pleading with God for any specific request?

2. Have there been times in your life when God said "no" to your requests? How did you respond?

3. Have you ever sensed God leading you to do something difficult? How did you respond?

CHAPTER 4

HANNAH PRAYS FOR A CHILD

I have been pouring out my soul before the LORD.
(1 Samuel 1:15)

MOSES, THE GREAT PROPHET OF ISRAEL, DIED IN THE wilderness. Because of the incident recorded in Numbers 20, he was not allowed to enter the Promised Land. He was, however, charged with the task of preparing his protégé Joshua to lead Israel into the Promised Land. Joshua led miraculous victories at Jericho and against the Amorites (Joshua 6, 10). Joshua also oversaw disastrous failures at Ai and with the Gibeonites (Joshua 7, 9). But for the most part Joshua was a God-fearing man who encouraged Israel to follow the LORD. Unfortunately, just like Moses, Joshua died. After burying their 110 year-old general, the people of Israel had a home, but lacked a leader (Joshua 24:29).

Enter the period of the judges, one of the darkest and most tragic chapters in the history of Israel. A cursory reading through the book of Judges feels like an episode of the *Twilight Zone*. Even in the good times, things just seem a bit off. And in the bad times, depravity runs wild and unchecked. The problem began shortly after Joshua died. Without a strong leader constantly pointing Israel to the LORD, the people once again fell back into idolatry (Judges 2:11-15). At this point, the Bible describes a repeating cycle of despair, deliverance, and depravity.

Part of the problem was the fact that Israel intermarried with the idolatrous nations they were supposed to destroy, and these marriages resulted in religious compromise (Judges 3:6). Another part of the problem was the judges themselves! Ehud was an assassin. Deborah had to lead in battle because the men were too scared to fight. Gideon fashioned an idol on the heels of an amazing military victory. Jephthah murdered his own daughter just to keep a foolish vow. And don't forget the most famous judge of all, Samson, an alcoholic-womanizer. The character of these men and woman was less than stellar.

So part of the problem was intermarriage with idolatrous people. Part of the problem was lousy leadership (the judges themselves). But there was one more major problem. The book of Judges ends with this dilemma: "In those days there was no king in Israel. Everyone did what was right in his own eyes." (Judges 21:25) Morality was relative, and the author of Judges links this problem to the fact that Israel did not have a king.

By the time you read through Judges (and things only get worse as the book progresses), you have pretty much lost all hope for Israel. Thankfully the book of Ruth comes next. Ruth reminds us that even when disaster and calamity and wickedness seem to be running unchecked, God is working for the good of his people. His work may take place behind the scenes. His work may take place through unlikely people. But God is always working for the good of his people. Ruth ends with a wedding and a baby shower. Not only does Ruth marry Boaz (Ruth 4:13), Ruth also gives birth to a son named Obed (Ruth 4:17). The book of Ruth ends with this hopeful line, "Obed fathered Jesse, and Jesse fathered David." (Ruth 4:17) The king alluded to at the end of Judges is now on the horizon.

But the king was still a few generations away, and before David would sit on the throne of Israel, one more judge needed to take the stage. This judge was Samuel, and the story of his birth begins like so many good stories in the Bible, with a barren woman.

1 Samuel 1 introduces us to a man named Elkanah who was married to two women, Hannah and Peninnah (1 Samuel 1:1-2). Peninnah had been blessed with children while Hannah was unable to conceive (1 Samuel 1:2). The

tension between competing wives was exacerbated by the fact that one was able to provide her husband with offspring while the other was not. Roll that strain into the stress of a yearly family vacation to Shiloh, and you have the recipe for disaster (1 Samuel 1:3-8). On these trips, Peninnah was less than kind. She always made a point to mock Hannah for her barrenness. Elkanah made matters worse by trying to reason with his distraught wife, suggesting that he should more than make up for Hannah's lack of children (1 Samuel 1:8).

Hannah was not amused, and she had every reason in the world to turn inward with bitterness and cynicism. Instead, Hannah prayed. The prayers of this heartbroken woman offered to the LORD are among the most remarkable in Scripture. Take a moment to read the moving story in 1 Samuel 9-20. These verses are packed with lessons about prayer, seven of which will be mentioned here.

First, prayer is always an appropriate response when you are troubled and distressed. The Bible records Hannah was "provoked" by her rival (1 Samuel 1:6, 7). The Bible also records Hannah "wept and would not eat" because of her barrenness (1 Samuel 1:7). The Bible demonstrates Hannah was "deeply distressed ... and wept bitterly" (1 Samuel 1:10). The Bible even records Hannah's own description of her circumstances. According to Hannah, she was, "troubled in spirit ... speaking out of my great anxiety and vexation" (1 Samuel 1:15, 16). This troubled and distressed woman did not allow her circumstances to drive her away from the LORD. Instead, in her despair, she turned to the LORD in prayer.

Second, the deeper your trouble, the more fervently you should pray. Clearly Hannah was troubled, and her prayers were not routine, casual, or calm. Instead, Hannah prayed with such intensity that Eli the priest thought she was drunk (1 Samuel 1:13). In her own words, Hannah was, "pouring out my soul before the LORD" (1 Samuel 1:15). Deep trouble ought to result in fervent prayer.

Third, prayer does not have to be expressed verbally. Psalm 44:21 reminds us that God knows even the secrets of our heart. Psalm 139:4 reminds us that God knows our words even before they are spoken. Hannah understood these truths, and as she poured out her heart to the LORD she did it silently (1 Samuel 1:12-13). Eli the priest may have been confused, but God knew and God heard Hanna's prayer.

Fourth, when you bring your requests to God, leave them there trusting God to do what is best. After Hannah fervently made her request to the LORD, the Bible explains she "went her way and ate, and her face was no longer sad" (1 Samuel 1:18). Hannah made her request and left trusting God to do the right thing. She ate. She changed her countenance. And she went on with life. Her request had not been answered, nor had she been given any kind of promise about the future. But she trusted God to handle her situation, and she refused to let the uncertainty of her situation impact her day to day life.

Fifth, worship God regardless of how God answers your prayers. Again, Hannah left this prayer session without an answer or a promise for the future. But she also left with an abiding and confident trust in the God to whom she had prayed. Therefore, it is not surprising to read that, "They rose early in the morning and worshipped before the LORD; then they went back to their house at Ramah." (1 Samuel 1:19) Unlike to many people, Hannah refused to let her distress hinder her worship. Did she *feel* like worshipping? Was it an amazing worship *experience*? The Bible doesn't tell us. We do know that despite the uncertainty in her life, Hannah worshipped.

Sixth, it is okay to make a vow to God. In making her request for a child, Hannah made a vow. She vowed that if God would give her a child, she would in turn give the child back to God (1 Samuel 1:11). This is a remarkable vow, and it sheds light on the motivation behind Hannah's prayer. She didn't just want a child to get even with Peninnah. If revenge was her motivation, she would not have offered to give this child back to the LORD. Instead, Hannah was motivated by a genuine desire to have a child and by the accompanying heartbreak that comes from infertility. As a result, her vow reveals the selfless-ness of her heart. She offered to give back to God the very thing she asked from God.

Seventh, if you make a vow, keep it. The Bible tells us that Hannah did conceive and give birth to a son (1 Samuel 1:19-20). One wonders, after the LORD granted her request, was Hannah tempted to hang on to this gift? Did she think about keeping young Samuel, her firstborn, at home? The Bible doesn't detail the temptations she faced. The Bible does tell us that at the appropriate time, Hannah kept her vow and gave her son Samuel back to the LORD (1 Samuel 1:21-28).

At this point in the story, Hannah prayed once again (1 Samuel 2:1-10). This time Hannah's circumstance were different, and her prayer was different. Her prayer in chapter one is a prayer of distress and desperation. Her prayer in chapter two is a prayer of thanksgiving and rejoicing. It may be tempting to read the prayer of chapter two as a woman gloating because she got her way. But don't forget, Hannah's prayer in chapter two comes *after* Hannah has left her beloved son with Eli in Shiloh (1 Samuel 1:21-28). Just like her prayer of distress and desperation in chapter one, Hannah's prayer of thanksgiving and rejoicing in chapter two reveals the heart of a woman who trusted in the LORD. This is a woman who worshipped regardless of her circumstances.

In this prayer, Hannah confirms that her joy comes from the salvation of the LORD, not her circumstances (1 Samuel 2:1). Good theology results in good prayer, and Hannah's theology is put on display when she acknowledges God as holy and unique (1 Samuel 2:2). Hannah reminds herself of the danger of boasting and pride, and she reminds herself that God the Judge knows all things (1 Samuel 2:3). Having experienced both infertility and child birth, Hannah recognizes God as the ultimate reverser of fortunes (1 Samuel 2:4-5). Taking this idea further, Hannah confesses God's sovereignty over every area of life as the Creator of all things (1 Samuel 2:6-8). Hannah also expresses her confidence that God's people will stand while his enemies fall (1 Samuel 2:9-10).

The end of Hannah's second prayer is worth noting. She ends by referring to the "anointed" of the LORD (1 Samuel 2:10). This is the Hebrew word "Messiah," in Greek "Christ." Initially, Hannah may be referring to Samuel who was "anointed" to serve as a judge and prophet in Israel. Eventually, this may be a reference to David who was "anointed" to serve as king over Israel (after all, it was Hannah's son Samuel who was eventually called to anoint Jesse's youngest son as the future king, see 1 Samuel 16). But ultimately this is a reference to Jesus, the Messiah, the Christ who fulfills every aspect of Hannah's prayer in chapter two. Jesus brings salvation. Jesus is holy and unique. Jesus is the all-knowing Judge. Jesus is the ultimate reverser of fortunes. Jesus is the sovereign Creator. Jesus will stand with his people while his enemies bow at his feet.

With this prayer, Hannah fades into the background. She is never mentioned again in the Bible. But her example in prayer endures. Here is a woman who knew who she was and knew who God was. Here is a woman who was constant in prayer and faith and worship, regardless of the circumstance of her life.

Learning to Pray

When the doctor finally told Sara the bad news, all she could think was, "Four miscarriages in three years. Four miscarriages in three years. Four. The number rang in her ears."

In high school and college Sara was convinced that she never wanted to have kids. She had plans and dreams and ambition, and she didn't want kids to get in the way. Her plan was confirmed when Tim came along. Tim loved Jesus just like Sara did, but he certainly wasn't in any hurry to have kids. Going into marriage, Sara and Tim had every intention of remaining childless for years to come. The plan played out perfectly for a while. Sara and Tim enjoyed each other, enjoyed traveling, and enjoyed freedom.

Then the no child firewall began to crumble. Tim's brother had two kids, a boy and a girl. Much to their surprise, Sara and Tim loved being Aunt Sara and Uncle Tim. About the same time several of Sara's friends began having children. The final blow was a Sunday morning spent helping in the church nursery. At lunch after church Sara and Tim decided they were ready to have kids. The plan had changed.

In their exuberance, Sara and Tim never considered the possibility that they might not be able to have kids. Now they were three years down the road with four miscarriages behind them. The doctors were baffled. Everything seemed to be fine physically. But each pregnancy ended the same.

Tim was the first to fall, but Sara wasn't far behind. Bitterness was too hard to resist. Neither could understand why God was making them endure this nightmare. Tim's brother hadn't gone through anything like this, nor had any of Sara's friends. Everyone in their Sunday school class seemed to have normal pregnancies. In fact, it seemed like they saw pregnant women and babies everywhere they went. Everyone was having kids except them. Was God punishing them for not wanting kids for so long? Were they not fit to be parents? They knew the questions were silly, but they couldn't help but wonder. The truth is, Tim and Sara didn't do much praying at all after the third miscarriage. They stopped asking for a normal pregnancy because prayer hadn't helped yet. They also stopped asking, "Why?" because no answers had been given.

Thankfully Sara and Tim didn't give up on church, and the pastor's sermon on 1 Samuel 1-2 hit them both like a punch to the nose. They realized that they allowed tragedy to drive them away from God instead of toward God. They realized that their prayers had been filled with advice and instruction for God instead of trust in

God. They realized that they never prayed like Hannah prayed in 1 Samuel 2. Instead of simply questioning God and complaining to God, Sara and Tim began praying prayers of praise and adoration to God. They still prayed for a normal pregnancy and a healthy baby. But they stopped focusing on their requests and started focusing on God.

QUESTIONS FOR DISCUSSION

1. Are you allowing circumstances in your life to drive you away from God in anger or to God in prayer? Are you worshipping God before and regardless of how he answers your prayers?

2. When you pray, are you trusting God to do what is best? Or are you anxious and fretful about the outcome?

3. Think about Hanna's theology in 1 Samuel 2. How are these truths impacting your prayer life?

CHAPTER 5

DAVID'S PRAYER OF GRATITUDE

Who am I, O Lord GOD, and what is my house,
that you have brought me thus far? (2 Samuel
7:18)

THE STORY OF 1 SAMUEL FOCUSES ON THE TUMULTUOUS
reign of Saul, the first king of Israel. During Saul's reign,
we are introduced to David, who would eventually follow
Saul as Israel's king. All of the drama, intrigue, and con-
flict between these two men is detailed on the pages of 1
Samuel. In the end, Saul dies, and David lives.

2 Samuel begins where 1 Samuel left off. Saul is dead, and
eventually David assumes the throne of Israel (2 Samuel
1-6). David's life up to this point has been eventful to say
the least. He battled wild animals as a shepherd (1 Samuel 17:34). He defeated and beheaded a giant in mortal

combat (1 Samuel 17). He even survived life on a run as a fugitive (1 Samuel 19-31). By the time you get to 2 Samuel 7, David has finally been established as king over Israel and he has found a measure of rest (2 Samuel 7:1).

In this rest, David had time to be still and think. The king looked around and realized that while he was living in a beautiful home, the Ark of the Covenant was being housed in a tent (2 Samuel 7:2). This troubled David, and he decided the Ark of the Covenant needed to be placed in a house. When David asked Nathan about the possibility of such a building, Nathan encouraged him saying, "Go do all that is in your heart, for the LORD is with you." (2 Samuel 7:3).

Then God threw Nathan and David a curveball. God spoke to Nathan that very night and told him to deliver a message to David (2 Samuel 7:4). This message centered not on David's plans for God, but rather on God's plans for David. God began by reminding David that he did not need a house, he had never lived in a house, and he did not ask for a house (2 Samuel 7:4-7). Imagine David's surprise! He planned to do something nice for God, and God responded with, "Thanks, but no thanks." God proceeded to remind David that Israel had been blessed by God, and as king David himself had been blessed by God (2 Samuel 7:7-11). God was reminding David that as God, he needed no one to protect him or provide for him. Instead, God was the one who had faithfully and consistently protected and provided for his people.

Then came the biggest curveball of all. Instead of David building a house for God, God promised to build a house for David! The Bible records God's words of promise and commitment in 2 Samuel 7:11-16. One can only imagine David's shock at this point in the conversation. First, David learns that he is not going to build God a house. Second, David learns that God has plans to build David a "house." Third, David learns that God will raise up his offspring, establish his (David's offspring) kingdom, and allow him (David's offspring) to build God's house. Fourth, David learns that God's love will be with his "house" forever. All of these promises in response to David's plan to build a house for the Ark.

In response to these promises, David prayed. Take a minute to read David's prayer in 2 Samuel 7:18-29. Even from a man who prayed remarkably, this prayer stands out. This is the prayer of a man who understood three things. First, David understood who he was. Second, David understood who God was. Third, David understood the nature of his relationship with God. If you can master those three things, you can master prayer. Who are you? Who is God? What is the nature of your relationship? David understood that he was the creature who had nothing of significance to offer the Almighty. David understood that God was the one who had been and would always work on behalf of his people, not needing anything from them. David understood that his relationship with the LORD was entirely based on grace and mercy.

In particular, there are at least eight aspects of David's prayer in 2 Samuel 7:18-29 that are worth mentioning. Identifying the parts of David's prayer will not only help one's understanding of the Bible, it will also help one learn how to pray.

First, David approached God in prayer with appropriate humility. In verse 18 David asks the rhetorical question, "Who am I, O Lord GOD, and what is my house, that you have brought me thus far?" Elsewhere, David asked a similar question: "What is man that you are mindful of him, and the son of man that you care for him?" (Psalm 8:4) In Psalm 8, David's humility was motivated by the grandeur of creation. In 2 Samuel 7 David's humility was motivated by the grandeur of God's blessing. In both places, David responded to God in prayer with appropriate humility. This is not the kind of faux humility that tries to diminish the dignity of human beings. Rather, this is the kind of humility that arises in the heart of someone who has caught a glimpse of the greatness of God.

Second, David not only acknowledged the amazing blessing of God in his life, but he also acknowledged that blessing David was an easy thing for God to do. After reflecting on how far God had brought him (from the sheep fold to the throne), and after reflecting on the promises of God yet to unfold in his life (offspring who will rule an eternal kingdom) David simply confessed, "And yet this was a small thing in your eyes, O Lord GOD." (2 Samuel

7:19) David understood the omnipotence of God, and this understanding formed a firm foundation for his prayers.

Third, David rested in the grace of God. He understood that the blessing of God had been poured out into his life, not because of anything in his heart and not because of anything he had done. Rather God's blessing was simply a result of God's promises and God's heart (2 Samuel 2:20-21). In recognizing this through prayer, David reminded himself of and praised God for his marvelous, free, undeserved, unmerited grace.

Fourth, David recognized the greatness and uniqueness of God saying, "Therefore you are great, O LORD God. For there is none like you, and there is no God besides you, according to all that we have heard with our ears." (2 Samuel 7:22) David had lived in Canaan long enough to know the truth about the gods of other nations. While he was on the run and hiding from Saul, he spent time among the Philistines (2 Samuel 27). David knew that Baal and Asherah and Molech and Chemosh were gods who sat and waited for their subjects to work on their behalf. The LORD, on the other hand, was a God who worked on behalf of his people. This set the God of Israel apart from the other gods as unique, and David took time in prayer to recognize the uniqueness of the LORD.

Fifth, David confessed that Israel had been redeemed for God's glory. There was nothing worthy or deserving inherent in his nation or even his own heart. David knew that God had chosen and redeemed and sustained Israel to make a name for himself among the nations (2 Samuel 7:23). This is what set Israel apart from the nations. It was not their inherent goodness, but rather God's desire to bring glory to himself through these people.

Sixth, David expressed his faith that God had entered into a one-of-a-kind relationship with Israel. In 2 Samuel 7:24 David prayed, "And you established for yourself your people Israel to be your people forever. And you, O LORD, became their God." There is no suggestion that Israel chose the LORD, or that Israel had decided to bind themselves to the LORD. David clearly understood that God's sovereign grace was the deciding factor in the eternal relationship between God and his people. David clearly understood that it was this grace that provided the occasion for David to pray in the first place.

Eighth, David based his prayer on the revelation of God (2 Samuel 7:25-27). God had spoken and God had graciously given revelation to David, and only in response to this revelation did David find the courage to pray to the LORD (2 Samuel 7:27). David's entire prayer was a response to the words of God that David believed to be both true and good (2 Samuel 7:27-29). First God speaks, then we respond in prayer. It has always been—and will always be—this way.

Taken as a whole, David's prayer in 2 Samuel 7 is the prayer of a man who knows who he is, who knows who

God is, and who understands the nature of his relationship with God. Like David, if we can master these three things, we can master prayer.

LEARNING TO PRAY

Five months earlier Jake had accepted his pastor's challenge to read through the entire Bible. He ordered a Bible that laid out daily readings and jumped in with enthusiasm. Jake soared through Genesis and Exodus. He struggled through Leviticus and Numbers. He finally established a consistent habit somewhere in Deuteronomy. Now it was May and Jake was reading through 2 Samuel. As he read about David and his interactions with the God of Israel, Jake had a strange thought. If he was honest, he rarely prayed. When he did pray, his prayers were nothing like David's prayers. Jake was somewhat embarrassed to realize the only consistent prayer time in his life was before meals. Those prayers usually amounted to a brief word of thanks for food and a request that God would bless the food (whatever that meant).

Jake resolved to change his prayer life. First, he committed to spend more time in prayer. Second, he wanted to pray like David, a man after God's own heart. Since his current prayer life centered on meals, Jake decided to begin there, at the dinner table. He studied David's prayer in 2 Samuel 7, and he reached the following conclusions.

First, Jake concluded that his meal time prayers were far too casual. This was not a conversation between equals. Rather, this was a conversation between creature and Creator, between a sinner and the Holy One. This was not a conversation he was entitled to have. This was a conversation he was privileged to have. Jake wanted to approach God with appropriate reverence and humility, even in a simple meal time prayer.

Second, Jake noticed that much of David's prayer involved David telling God about God. Jake was ashamed to admit that he didn't know much about the character and nature of God. But if he was ever going to pray like David, he knew he needed to learn. Jake wanted his prayers to be more than a request from a stranger. He resolved to study and learn about God's characteristics and attributes.

Third, Jake saw that David's prayer was a response to God's promises. First God talked. Then David talked. Applying this to his own life, Jake realized his six-month old Bible reading habit was crucial to his prayer life. He needed to hear from God each day in order to respond appropriately in prayer. Jake had spent the first five months of the year reading God's Word. Now he committed to spend the rest of the year reading and responding in prayer. Whether he was alone, with his family, or with coworkers ... Whether it was before work, before a meal, or before bed ... Jake wanted to pray like a man after God's own heart.

Questions for Discussion

1. How does your understanding of your sinfulness impact your prayer life?

2. How do your beliefs about God's character and grace impact your prayer life?

3. David's prayer was a response to God's revealed promises. How are you allowing God's revealed promises to impact your prayer life?

CHAPTER 6

SOLOMON'S TEMPLE PRAYER

Heaven and the highest heaven cannot contain
you; how much less this house that I have built!
(1 Kings 8:27)

AFTER HE HAD BEEN ESTABLISHED AS KING OVER ISRAEL, and after he enjoyed a period of rest from all his enemies, David began to dream about a majestic building project (2 Samuel 7:1-2). This project would be a beautiful temple to house the Ark of the Covenant, the very throne of the LORD, which was currently housed in a tent. David pitched his idea to the prophet Nathan, who encouraged David saying, "Go, do all that is in your heart, for the LORD is with you." (2 Samuel 6:3) What David and Nathan did not know, but quickly found out, is that David would not be the one to build this great temple. Instead, it would be David's yet to be conceived son Solomon who would lead this building project.

While he was certainly disappointed that he would not be the one to build the temple, David made ample preparation for Solomon. The Bible records David purchased land and assembled a "great quantity" of materials for the project (1 Chronicles 21:18-22:5). With everything in place, and knowing his life was coming to an end, David summoned Solomon and charged the future king to, "build a house for the LORD, the God of Israel (1 Chronicles 22:6).

Upon David's death, Solomon assumed the throne of Israel (1 Kings 2:13-46). Solomon began his reign with a humble prayer asking for wisdom to lead the nation that ultimately belonged to the LORD (1 Kings 3:1-15). The Bible demonstrates God was pleased with this request, and in addition to wisdom, Solomon was granted great power and great wealth (1 Kings 3:10-14). Solomon's wisdom and greatness are described in the following chapters leading up to this summary of his early reign: "People of all nations came to hear the wisdom of Solomon, and from all the kings of the earth, who had heard of his wisdom." (1 Kings 4:34) In the midst of this greatness, Solomon began to work on the project his father had envisioned. He began building a temple for the LORD.

In the midst of construction, God spoke to Solomon saying, "Concerning this house that you are building, if you will walk in my statutes and obey my rules and keep all my commandments and walk in them, then I will establish my word with you, which I spoke to David your father. And I will dwell among the children of Israel and will not forsake my people Israel." (1 Kings 6:12-13)

These words were a reminder of God's previous promises and an encouragement to the young king. Solomon continued in the work, and the temple was finished seven years later (1 Kings 6:14, 38). With the physical construction complete, Solomon began to plan a grand dedication service. He assembled the people of Israel, he called on the Levites to carry the Ark into its new home, and he offered a multitude of sacrifices (1 Kings 8:1-11). When the Ark was in place, the glory of the God of Israel filled the temple, causing the priests standing by to fall on their faces (1 Kings 8:11).

At this point, Solomon prayed. With the king and the priests and the elders and the people absolutely overwhelmed by the glorious presence of their God, Solomon stopped to talk to the LORD. The first thing to note about Solomon's prayer is the fact that it was corporate prayer. Several times the Bible reminds us that Solomon stood in front of the gathered assembly and led the people in prayer (1 Kings 8:1-2, 14, 22, 55). While there is always a place for personal, private prayer (see the example of Hannah in 1 Samuel 1-2, or the teaching of Jesus in Matthew 6:5-6), corporate prayer is special. In both the Old Testament and the New Testament, God's people gathering together to talk to God as an assembled people is special. Some of the corporate prayers in Scripture are led by kings, others by apostles. But the example set forth in Scripture is clear—corporate prayer is important and should be a regular part of our prayer lives.

Solomon's actual prayer as he stood before Israel can be found in 1 Kings 8:12-61. Take a few minutes to read Solomon's lengthy prayer in 1 Kings 8:12-61, and note these seven lessons about prayer.

First, in verses 12-21, Solomon began by acknowledging the promises God made to David. In other words, like his father before him, Solomon prayed in response to revelation from God. In the grand scheme of things, all prayer is a response to prior revelation from God. In the beginning God spoke and created the heavens and the earth (Genesis 1). It was God who spoke to Adam and Eve in the beginning (Genesis 1:28-30). Creation itself testifies to the existence and the power and the goodness of God (Psalm 19, Romans 1). This understanding must always shape our prayers. God speaks first, and we respond. Until we have listened to the Word of God, we are in no position to speak.

Second, in verses 22-26, Solomon reflected on the absolute uniqueness of the LORD. All around Israel there were nations devoted to various gods and goddesses. Solomon was aware of this idolatry, and he understood that the God of Israel stood out as unique among the many "gods" of the peoples. According to this portion of

Solomon's prayer, the God of Israel was unique because he alone was a promise-making and promise-keeping God. Solomon's prayer not only acknowledged the promises of God, but it was entirely based on the promises of God. Our prayers must always begin with the promises of God, and our prayers must ultimately express faith in the God who keeps his promises.

Third, in verses 27-30, Solomon reminded himself and the people of two theological truths. One, despite the grandeur of the temple before them, no building could contain the fullness of the glory of God. Two, the presence of God was truly made manifest in the temple. These truths taken together provided an important balance for the people of Israel. Their God was both transcendent and immanent. He filled the heavens above, and yet chose to dwell with Israel in the temple. He was not contained by the temple, but he really did manifest his presence in the temple. These truths not only provided balance for the ancient Israelites who found themselves in an idolatrous context, they also laid the foundation for a New Covenant understanding of the incarnation. This in turn impacts our prayers as believers. We pray to the God who created and sustains all things, and this same God took on humanity to dwell with us (John 1:1-2, 14).

Fourth, in verses 31-53, Solomon runs through a series of hypothetical situations, all of which eventually came to pass. If an individual sins against a neighbor (1 Kings 8:31-32) ... If Israel is defeated in battle because of sin (1

Kings 8:33-34) ... If there is no rain because of sin (1 Kings 8:35-36) ... If there is a famine or plague in the land (1 Kings 8:37-40) ... If foreigners come to the temple to worship (1 Kings 8:41-43) ... If Israel loses in battle (1 Kings 8:44-45) ... If Israel is guilty of corporate sin against God (1 Kings 8:46-53) ... For each of these hypotheticals that eventually became reality, Solomon preemptively asked God to hear the prayers that would be offered by his people. Basically, Solomon prayed that God would hear future prayers. In praying this, Solomon acknowledged that the prayers of Israel did not place the LORD at the mercy of the people (as was believed by many of the animistic cultures around Israel). Instead, Solomon understood that Israel always remained at the mercy of their God. Such an understanding must always shape our prayers. In prayer we are not controlling God, advising God, or manipulating God to do our bidding.

Fifth, in verse 54 we read that throughout this prayer Solomon had knelt on his knees and lifted his hands toward heaven. His posture revealed the emotion of his heart. Kneeling showed his humility before God. Lifting his hands showed his desire to receive from God. Solomon was the one in need. God was the one supplying that need.

Sixth, in verses 55-61, Solomon prayed a prayer of benediction, or blessing, over the congregation. This was a prayer spoken out loud, to God, for the benefit of the people. Solomon asked God to keep his promises, and Solomon asked God to keep his people faithful. While there is great value in this sort of prayer, there is a warning in the story that follows. This leads us to the final point.

In the chapters that follow we are reminded that a good prayer life today does not ensure a God honoring life tomorrow. Solomon's prayer in 1 Kings 8 is noteworthy for its God-centered content, its basis in the revealed promises of God, and its humble tone. These same characteristics initially marked the reign of Solomon, and 1 Kings 9 and 10 mark the high point of Israel as a nation. The temple was complete. The king was devoted to the God of his people. And the nations recognized the blessing of God in the prosperity of Israel. Then we read 1 Kings 11, a chapter that marks the beginning of the end for Solomon and Israel. The faith and spirituality that produced the moving prayer of 1 Kings 8 was eventually replaced by an idolatrous love of women and their gods. Let the reader pay heed, a good prayer life today does not ensure a God-honoring life tomorrow.

LEARNING TO PRAY

It was the first night back from the hospital, and the house was finally still. All the kids were asleep in bed. Amy and Lance knew from experience that the hospital was no place for new parents to rest, so they were relieved to be home. Everyone was healthy. Everyone was asleep. Everyone was quiet.

As they sat in the dimly lit living room, Amy and Lance talked about their kids. Emily was eight, Nicole was five, Annie was three, and now they had Cade. Each kid was unique. They had different personalities and different abilities. Amy and Lance dreamed out loud about what the future held for their kids. The possibilities were exciting, but they were also frightening. Amy and Lance were not naïve. They knew the world was a tough, broken place. They knew their kids would have to navigate many temptations in life.

No one had to tell Amy and Lance to pray for their kids. They prayed instinctively from the first day Amy found out she was pregnant with Emily. They prayed about anything they couldn't control, especially about the future. At times it seemed like they were planning life for their kids and advising God about the best possible outcome. At times it seemed like they were asking God to make everything easy for their kids. Keep them healthy. Keep them comfortably middle class. Keep them from marital trouble. Keep them from anything that would bring pain into their lives.

As she sat in the dark living room, Amy found herself questioning these kinds of prayers. She was fairly certain her parents prayed these same prayers for her over the last thirty years. She also knew her own life had not been pain-free. There had been hard times in her marriage. There had been financial struggles. There had been times of sin and rebellion. God had certainly been faithful through it all, but there had been pain.

In addition to her own experience, Amy couldn't shake 1 Kings 11 from her mind. She came across the passage in a Bible study at church. In these verses Amy saw a man pray humbly, with his face on the ground. Solomon's posture revealed position of his heart, and Amy knew that most of her prayers lacked genuine humility. She knew she had been guilty of treating God as a genie who grants wishes instead of the sovereign Lord of the universe. She resolved to stop coming to God with advice.

Amy also resolved to stop asking God to keep her children from any and all pain. Instead, she decided to use 1 Kings 11 as a model for prayer. Like Solomon praying for Israel, Amy knew her kids would make bad decisions. They would rebel. They would stray. So instead of praying that God would make everything easy, she started praying that God would be merciful when her children repented. She actually prayed for the future prayers of her children, asking God to hear their cries for mercy and respond with grace.

QUESTIONS FOR DISCUSSION

1. How do the doctrines of transcendence and immanence impact your prayer life?

2. Have you been guilty of assuming your prayers somehow controlled God, or put God as your disposal? How can you correct this mistake?

3. Is there a time when your physical posture (bowing, raising hands, etc.) reveals the position of your heart in prayer?

CHAPTER 7

ELIJAH STRUGGLES IN PRAYER

It is enough; now, O LORD, take away my life.
(1 Kings 19:4)

THE BOOK OF JAMES GIVES REMARKABLE INSIGHT INTO the prayer life of the great prophet Elijah. James 5:17-18 explains Elijah controlled the weather with his prayers. He prayed, and it did not rain. For three and half years not a drop fell from the sky. Elijah prayed again, and it rained. This New Testament insight about the power of Elijah's prayer life makes 1 Kings 19:4 all the more shocking. In 1 Kings 19:4 Elijah prayed to God and asked him to take his life. It's a suicide prayer. The previous three verses indicate that Elijah prayed this prayer because Jezebel, the wife of King Ahab, had taken out a contract on Elijah's head. The Bible shows Elijah was afraid and asked God to kill him (1 Kings 19:3).

How does this happen? How does a prayer-warrior like Elijah find himself running from the queen, hiding in the wilderness, and praying for death? The back story found in 1 Kings 17-19 is both illuminating and perplexing. Illuminating because it explains the events that led up to Elijah's spiritual collapse. Perplexing because it describes events that should have bolstered Elijah's faith. The back story begins with Ahab.

We meet Ahab in 1 Kings 16:29-33. Twice we are told that Ahab was more wicked and rebellious than any king who came before him (1 Kings 16:30, 33). He married a Sidonian princess named Jezebel who worshipped pagan gods (1 Kings 16:31). This resulted in Ahab bringing Baal worship and Asherah worship into the capital city of Samaria (1 Kings 16:31). To summarize, "Ahab did more to provoke the LORD, the God of Israel, to anger than all the kings of Israel who were before him." (1 Kings 16:33)

Enter Elijah. His name appears for the first time in 1 Kings 17:1 in contrast to Ahab. The rivalry between these men kicked off with Elijah telling Ahab that the LORD would not send rain on Israel until Elijah prayed for rain (1 Kings 17:1). You can imagine this did not sit well with wicked Ahab, so the LORD told Elijah to hit the road. Elijah camped out east of the Jordan River, and the LORD commanded a flock of ravens to provide his fugitive prophet with food (1 Kings 17:3-7). Note these two miracles. First, Elijah prayed and the rain stopped. Second, God provided safety and food for Elijah. Elijah was beginning to learn about the power of prayer and the provision of God.

The two stories that follow confirm the lessons God was teaching Elijah. First is the story about oil and flour. God sent Elijah to a foreign country where he met a destitute widow (1 Kings 17:8-10). This widow had reached a dead end in life, and she was literally preparing to die (1 Kings 17:12). Elijah told her that if she fed him first, she would not run out of oil or flour until the day God sent rain on the earth (1 Kings 17:14). The widow did what Elijah told her to do, and the newly formed trio of Elijah, the widow, and her son had oil and flour for three and a half years. Again, Elijah was learning about the power of prayer and the provision of God.

The second story in 1 Kings 17 is related to the first. It is a story about death. At some point in time the widow's son died (1 Kings 17:17). The Bible records Elijah cried out to the LORD about the widow's son (1Kings 17:20). Three times he stretched himself out on top of the dead child, crying out to the LORD to bring the child back to life (1 Kings 17:21). The Bible records, "And the LORD listened to the voice of Elijah. And the life of the child came into him again and he revived." (1 Kings 17:22)

First Elijah controlled the weather. Then he was fed by a flock of ravens. Then he saw the miracle of oil and flour.

Then he saw the dead raised. Elijah was continuing to learn about the power of prayer and the provision of God. As great as these miracles were, they were nothing compared to the miracle of 1 Kings 18. After three and a half years with no rain the famine in Samaria was severe, and Ahab decided it was time to talk to Elijah (1 Kings 18:3-6). The LORD agreed, and he sent Elijah to visit with Ahab (1 Kings 18:1-2). Elijah challenged Ahab to a showdown, telling his nemesis to bring the 450 prophets of Baal along with the 400 prophets of Asherah to Mount Carmel (1 Kings 18:19-20).

The story that follows is nothing short of spectacular. Elijah challenged the 850 pagan prophets of Jezebel to see if their gods could send fire from heaven (1 Kings 18:21-24). The Bible demonstrates these 850 prophets sang and danced from morning to noon, begging their gods to send fire (1 Kings 18:26). Not surprisingly, "There was no voice, and no one answered." (1 Kings 18:26) About noon, Elijah began mocking his opponents. He told them to yell louder, suggesting that their god was on a journey or taking a nap or possibly even using the restroom (1 Kings 18:27). Don't miss the humor in Elijah's sarcasm, and don't miss the courage with which he spoke. He is standing in front of 850 people who would love to see him dead, and he has the courage to mock them for their foolish idolatry. This is a man who has learned from droughts and ravens and oil and flour and death. This is a man who knows about the power of prayer and the provision of God.

The 850 prophets continued with their pleas, dancing and raving and even cutting themselves with knives. Again, "There was no voice. No one answered; no one paid attention." (1 Kings 18:29) Finally Elijah took the stage. He drenched his offering in water, proving that what was about to happen was no conjuror's trick (1 Kings 18:33-35). Elijah prayed to the God of Abraham, Isaac, and Jacob, asking him to show the people that he was the one true God (1 Kings 18:36-37). After Elijah prayed, the Bible records, "The fire of the LORD fell and consumed the burnt offering and the wood and the stones and the dust, and licked up the water that was in the trench." (1 Kings 18:38) Again, Elijah experienced first-hand the power of prayer and the provision of God.

After executing the 850 prophets of Baal and Asherah, it was time for rain. Elijah climbed Mount Carmel, bowed down on the ground and prayed (1 Kings 18:42). In a matter of moments, a downpour came upon the land (1 Kings 18:45-46). Add this to Elijah's life experience list. First the drought. Then the ravens. Then the oil and flour. Then the dead raised. Then the fire from heaven. Then the rain. In the most spectacular ways, Elijah had learned to trust in the power of prayer and the provision of God.

You would expect that at this point in his life, Elijah would be on the ultimate spiritual high. Then you turn to 1 Kings 19. In 1 Kings 19:3 we read that the bold, fearless, courageous prophet was afraid because Jezebel had promised to kill him (1 Kings 19:1-3). This makes no sense.

He just faced down and slaughtered 850 false prophets, and now Elijah is scared of a death threat from Jezebel? I struggle to understand Elijah's thought process here. Maybe Elijah was tired after a marathon run to Jezreel (1 Kings 18:46). Maybe Elijah was frustrated by the fact that even after God sent fire from heaven the people did not repent (1 Kings 19:4). Maybe Elijah was despondent because he felt like he was the last man on earth who trusted the LORD (1 Kings 19:10). Maybe we just need to remember that Elijah was a man with a fickle nature like ours (James 5:17-18). Or maybe there is another explanation for Elijah's fear.

In 1 Kings 19:4 Elijah prays this prayer, "It is enough; now, O LORD, take away my life, for I am no better than my fathers." This is a bold thing to pray, especially when you know the power of prayer like Elijah knew the power of prayer. God could control the weather, multiply food, raise the dead, and send fire from heaven. Surely God could take Elijah's life when he prayed for death. But instead of death, God sent an angel to feed Elijah, strengthening him for a 40 day journey to the mountain of God (1 Kings 19:5-8).

When Elijah arrived at the mountain of God, the LORD asked him a strange question. Having sent Elijah to the mountain, God asked Elijah, "What are you doing here, Elijah?" (1 Kings 19:9). The obvious answer was, "God, I am your servant, you sent me here, so I'm here." Instead of the obvious answer, Elijah responded out of the frustration of his heart (19:10). He looked around and saw no results from his labor. No one repented. No one turned back to the LORD. And Elijah assumed he was the only follower of Yahweh.

So, God sent Elijah to stand on the mountain. God sent a powerful wind that broke the rocks apart. God sent a terrifying earthquake that shook the mountain. God sent a fire that that threatened to consume the mountain. Strangely, the Bible shows God was not in the wind or the earthquake or the fire (1 Kings 19:11-12). Instead, God was in the sound of a "low whisper" (1 Kings 19:12). For years I have been puzzled by this story. What was God trying to teach his discouraged prophet? And what about the unanswered question of why Elijah would be afraid of Jezebel and pray for death? I believe the answer is obvious when you consider Elijah's experiences with God up to this point. Elijah had the opportunity to experience some of the most amazing miracles recorded in the Bible. Not only that, but he also had the privilege of participating in these miracles through prayer. God used Elijah's prayers to control the weather, multiply food, raise the dead, and send fire from heaven. Elijah had come to expect the miraculous and the spectacular when he prayed.

I believe this explains Elijah's fear of Jezebel, his prayer for death, and his experience on the mountain of God. We know Elijah was a man of prayer. It's logical to assume that he prayed when Jezebel threatened to kill him. And I believe Elijah expected another spectacular miracle to come from the LORD. Maybe a lightning bolt would hit Jezebel? Maybe a lion would devour Jezebel? Instead, nothing happened and Elijah was forced to run for his life. Despondent, he begged for death and complained to God that he was alone in his faith (1 Kings 19:4, 10, 14). God responded with a strong wind and a powerful earthquake and a raging fire. All were spectacular and miraculous. None contained the presence of God. Instead, God was in the still small voice.

God was trying to teach Elijah that prayer does not put God at our command. And while God certainly hears our prayers, and while he can respond with the spectacular and miraculous, sometimes God chooses to answer with a low whisper. There would be no spectacular miracle delivering Elijah from the threats of Jezebel. Instead, a low voice called Elijah to continue his prophetic ministry (1 Kings 19:15-18).

May we pray with the boldness of Elijah. May we remember that God can and does respond in spectacular and miraculous ways. But may we never forget that our prayers never put God at our command. And as we wait for God, may we be satisfied with the spectacular, the miraculous, the mundane, the ordinary, and even the low whisper.

LEARNING TO PRAY

David and Mary had been married for 48 years. The early years of their marriage were predictable. David finished pharmacy school. Mary stayed home with their two kids. They took vacations. They built a new house outside of town. David even opened his own pharmacy. Life was good.

No one was surprised when Mary began having trouble remembering things. The only surprise was how young she was when it started happening. Her father struggled with dementia, but his problems began later in life. Mary was 46 when she started getting lost and misplacing things. She knew what was coming, and so did David.

The early years were the worst. Mary knew enough to know she was losing her memory, and she worried about her family. David would have to work less to take care of her, or put her in an assisted living facility. Her children would not be able to have a normal relationship with their mother. Her grandchildren would only remember her as the lady who couldn't remember anything. Ironically, Mary's physical health was great. Unfortunately, it was only a matter of months before she had trouble remember three minutes ago. Most of the time Mary knew who David was. Everyone else was a stranger.

David's plans of retirement and grandkids and travel took a twist. Early retirement came about because he had to stay home with Mary. Grandkids were great, but they struggled to relate to a woman who couldn't remember their name. Travel amounted to quick trips to the grocery store while Mary napped. Mary needed David to be with her constantly, and he was glad to stay home and take care of his wife.

Things went on like this for almost 20 years. It was a lonely time for David. Friendships were neglected because David couldn't leave Mary alone, and he certainly couldn't take her out in a crowd. David's church involvement waned because he could only leave Mary for an hour for worship. The extra hour for small group was just too long to leave her alone. Through it all, David did his best to put on a brave face, but his spiritual life felt like a roller coaster. He felt like he was endlessly moving through the stages of grief. He regularly prayed for healing, at times begging, at times sobbing, and at times angry. But healing never came. Mary passed away peacefully at home almost 20 years later.

Somewhere in the midst of this trial, David began to take comfort in the story of Elijah. This fearless prophet complained and fretted about Jezebel five minutes after calling down fire from heaven. The lesson Elijah had to learn was simple. Sometimes God answers prayer miraculously with fire from heaven. Sometimes God answers prayer with a still small promise to be with his suffering servants. David took refuge in the truth that God was with him in the miraculous and the mundane. He refused to question God's plan. He refused to question

God's goodness. Instead, he regularly prayed that the still small promise would sustain him through grief.

Questions for Discussion

1. What life situations have taught you about the power of prayer and the provision of God?

2. Have you seen God do the miraculous in response to your prayers? Do you expect God to do the miraculous in response to your prayers?

3. Will you be content if God responds to your prayers in an ordinary way instead of a miraculous way?

CHAPTER 8

HEZEKIAH PRAYS FOR DELIVERANCE

So now, O LORD our God, save us please, from his hand, that all the kingdoms of the earth may know that you, O LORD, are God alone. (2 Kings 19:19)

THE KINGS OF ISRAEL STAND OUT FOR MANY REASONS. The first king of Israel was Saul. His reign was rocky to say the least. The second king of Israel was David. Without a doubt he was the greatest king of Israel. After David, Solomon assumed the throne. Solomon oversaw the zenith of Israel as well as the beginning of decline. After Solomon, things went downhill—and fast. Jeroboam and Rehoboam split the kingdom in two (1 Kings 12:16-24). Jeroboam ruled Israel in the north. Rehoboam ruled Judah in the South. For the most part, Israel's kings were hell bent on worshipping the gods of all the nations around Israel instead of the God of Israel. Judah's kings were a mixed bunch. Many are described as evil. Others loved God and actually tried to encourage Judah to follow the LORD.

One of the God-fearing kings of Judah was Hezekiah, who we meet in 2 Kings 18. The Bible reveals Hezekiah was 25 years old when he assumed the throne, and he reigned for 29 years (2 Kings 18:2). For the most part, Hezekiah did what right in the eyes of the LORD (2 Kings 18:3). This involved removing the high places of pagan worship and destroying various idols. He even broke the bronze serpent made by Moses in the wilderness many years earlier (2 Kings 18:4). In all these efforts, Hezekiah was desperately trying to remove idolatry from Judah. For all these efforts, Hezekiah distinguished himself as a remarkable, God-fearing king (2 Kings 18:5-6).

Towards the end of Hezekiah's story in 2 Kings 18, almost as an afterthought, we read this in verse 7: "He rebelled against the king of Assyria and would not serve him." This rebellion eventually resulted in one of the most dramatic scenes recorded in the Bible.

Immediately after introducing us to Hezekiah, the Bible describes how Shalmanaser king of Assyria conquered the Northern Kingdom of Israel. The siege lasted three years, and in the sixth year of Hezekiah's reign the capital city of Samaria fell to Assyria (2 Kings 18:10). Shalmanaser carried many Israelites into exile, and God allowed it all to happen because the people of Israel would neither listen to nor obey him (2 Kings 18:11-12).

Shalmanaser's reign over Assyria came to an end, and Sennacherib was made king. Eight years after the fall of Samaria, Sennacherib set his sights on the Southern Kingdom of Judah (2 Kings 18:13). Hezekiah decided that his earlier rebellion wasn't such a great idea, and offered to pay Sennacherib to leave without besieging Jerusalem (2 Kings 18:14-18). Sennacherib was not interested in Hezekiah's bribe, and he vowed to destroy both Hezekiah and Jerusalem (2 Kings 18:19-35). In his threats, Sennacherib even mocked Yahweh, the LORD, the God of Israel, suggesting that his power was no greater than the gods of Hamath, Arpad, Sepharvaim, Hena, or Ivvah (2 Kings 18:34).

When Hezekiah learned that Sennacherib had refused his bribe, and when Hezekiah learned that Sennacherib had vowed to destroy the city, he was distraught (2 Kings 19:1). In his distress, Hezekiah did what a God-fearing king should do. He called for a prophet (Isaiah) and asked him to pray for the nation (2 Kings 19:3-4). Isaiah not only prayed for Judah, he also sent word to Hezekiah that Sennacherib would soon be leaving Judah (2 Kings 19:6-7). Specifically, God said this through Isaiah, "I will put a spirit in him, so that he shall hear a rumor and return to his own land, and I will make him fall by the sword in his own land." (2 Kings 19:7)

87

Surprise, surprise ... About that time, Sennacherib heard a rumor from home. Tirhakah king of Cush had opportunistically attacked while the Assyrian army was deployed in Judah (2 Kings 19:9). Sennacherib made plans to return and defend his territory, but before going home he sent a final warning to Hezekiah. Sennacherib saw the attack of Cush as a coincidence, and he warned Hezekiah about thinking Yahweh had saved Israel (2 Kings 19:10-13). Sennacherib promised Hezekiah that Israel's fate would be no different than the other nations who had fallen before his army.

Despite Isaiah's reassurance, Hezekiah was unsure. When the king received this last message from Sennacherib he went to the temple to pray. Hezekiah took the message from the king of Assyria and spread it out before the LORD. Take a moment to read Hezekiah's moving prayer in 2 Kings 19:15-19.

This prayer can be broken down into four simple parts. First, Hezekiah firmly fixed his eyes on Yahweh, the LORD, the God of Israel (2 Kings 19:15). Instead of focusing on the dilemma before him, Hezekiah reminded himself that his God was on heaven's throne. His God was the only God. His God was the Creator. Second, Hezekiah asked God to hear the blasphemy of Sennacherib (2 Kings 19:16). He was obviously concerned that Sennacherib was threatening to destroy Judah. But he was also concerned that the one true God was being mocked by a foreign king. So, out of concern for

God's name, Hezekiah prayed that God would hear the mockery of Sennacherib. Third, Hezekiah acknowledged the reality of his dilemma, and the danger that stood before Judah (2 Kings 19:17-18). Assyria had destroyed many nations, and the gods of these nations had not been able to stop the Assyrian army. Hezekiah didn't minimize his problem. He didn't try to make himself feel better by telling him that other people had it worse than he did. Instead he honestly assessed the direness of his circumstances. Finally, Hezekiah asked God to save Judah from the Assyrian threat (2 Kings 19:19). This request was not motivated by Hezekiah's desire to be safe and comfortable. Instead, Hezekiah's request was motivated by a desire that, "all the kingdoms of the earth may know that you, O LORD, are God alone." (2 Kings 19:19)

After Hezekiah prayed this prayer, Isaiah the prophet once again sent a message to his king. Isaiah assured Hezekiah that the God of Israel had heard his prayer (2 Kings 19:20). Isaiah also reminded Hezekiah that God's plans were not being frustrated. Despite the boisterous bullying of Assyria, God's plans were being brought to perfect fulfillment just as it had been "determined" and "planned" long ago (2 Kings 19:25). Isaiah promised Hezekiah that God would put a hook in Sennacherib's nose and drag him back to Assyria (2 Kings 19:28).

One important detail worth noting is God's motivation for protecting Hezekiah and Judah. It may be tempting to assume that God was moved to pity by Hezekiah's prayer. While God did hear Hezekiah's prayer, he was not manipulated to action by Hezekiah's prayer (2 Kings 19:20). It may be tempting to assume that God was moved to pity because of the plight of his beloved people. While God did know the plight of his people, he was not moved to action because of any inherent goodness in the people of Judah. Rather, God was motivated to save his people by a desire to protect his reputation. God was outraged at the blasphemy of Sennacherib (2 Kings 19:28), and God chose to defend Jerusalem for the sake of his own name (2 Kings 19:34).

2 Kings 19 ends just as God promised it would end. In what might be the most understated verse of the Bible we read, "That night the angel of the LORD went out and struck down 185,000 in the camp of the Assyrians." (2 Kings 19:35) 185,000! The mighty Assyrian army was absolutely devastated by the angel of the LORD! With a decimated army, Sennacherib returned to Assyria, hook in nose. In his ignorance, he returned home and continued worshipping Nisroch, the Assyrian god of agriculture. In the midst of his worship, Sennacherib was murdered by his sons Adrammelech and Sharezer (2 Kings 19:37) He fell by the sword, just like God promised in 2 Kings 19:7.

In the midst of this remarkable story is the humble prayer of a God-fearing king. Hezekiah was certainly frightened by the massive horde that threatened to overrun his kingdom. And despite the reassurances of Isaiah, Hezekiah prayed. His prayer was a God-honoring petition, asking God to defend Judah for the sake of God's own name. The pattern of Hezekiah's prayer is simple. First, he praised God. Second, he asked God to listen and see. Third, he confessed the reality of his situation. Fourth, he asked God to act so that people would know the truth about God.

This simple pattern could be applied to many of the situations that move us to prayer. Think about your prayers for your unbelieving family and unbelieving friends. Think about your prayers for your country and your community. Think about your prayers for your church and your family. When you pray, use Hezekiah's prayer as a model. Begin with praise to God. Ask God to listen and see the situation. Confess the reality of the circumstances. And ask God to act so that people would know him and his glory.

LEARNING TO PRAY

Jay just returned from another mission trip. He had been on trips to Africa and South America, but nothing he had ever seen could prepare him for China. The mass of humanity. The massive buildings. The pervasive lostness. It was all too much to take in. Two months later Jay found himself still wrestling with the experience. He wondered why he had been born in Los Angeles instead of Beijing. He did not expect an answer to this question. He wondered how the gospel would be shared with the millions he saw. He hoped someone had an answer to this question. He wondered about the fate of the many faces he saw. He prayed for the gospel to run wild in China.

In addition to these questions, Jay began to think about his prayer life. Before his trip to China, Jay thought he had pretty much figured out the spiritual disciplines of Bible reading and prayer. Each morning he woke up early to read God's Word and pray for the things on his heart. He prayed for his kids, asking God make them healthy and successful. He prayed for his marriage, asking God to bless and protect his wife. He prayed for his job, asking God to bless his work and provide for his needs (and some of his wants).

But after returning from China, Jay began to feel uneasy about his prayer life. He realized that he spent most his time praying for four people while there were over a billion people in China he never prayed for. He realized that he spent most of his time praying for the comfort of his family while there were over a billion people in China who did not know the name of Jesus. Jay knew his prayer life needed to change. He knew he wanted to pray bigger prayers, selfless prayers, and global prayers. But he didn't know where to start. He was still overwhelmed with his experience in China.

A few weeks later Jay found a template for prayer in 2 Kings 19. Hezekiah's prayer was prayed at a different time and under different circumstances. But the structure gave direction to Jay as he prayed for China. First,

Jay resolved to begin every prayer by fixing his eyes on God. Instead of jumping into his many requests, Jay wanted to spend time declaring truth about the God to whom he prayed. Second, Jay consistently asked God to see the needs he saw in China. This wasn't an attempt to update God on something that had slipped his attention. Rather, it was an attempt to ask God to redeem a broken situation. Third, Jay acknowledged the size of the problem before him. He knew he would never be able to reach the masses of people he saw in China, but he believed God was up to the task. Finally, Jay prayed that God would act to change things in China. He prayed that God would raise up missionaries and indigenous pastors. He prayed that churches would grow and multiply. He prayed that God would bring glory to himself among the people of China.

QUESTIONS FOR DISCUSSION

1. In a crisis, how can you focus on God instead of your circumstances?

2. What drives the requests you make of God? Selfishness? Or a desire to see God glorified?

3. How does God's supreme desire to glorify himself impact your prayer life?

CHAPTER 9

JEHOSHAPHAT PRAYS
FOR DELIVERANCE

O our God, will you not execute judgment on them? For we are powerless against this great horde that is coming against us. We do not know what to do, but our eyes are on you (2 Chronicles 20:12)

THE PREVIOUS CHAPTER CENTERED ON A PRAYER OF Hezekiah, king of Judah. This chapter centers on a prayer of Jehoshaphat, king of Judah. Jehoshaphat was king of Judah long before Hezekiah took the throne. Despite the decades that separated Jehoshaphat and Hezekiah, these two men had several things in common. Both ruled as king over Judah. Both are described as good, God-fearing kings. And both prayed to the God of Israel when foreign armies marched against Jerusalem. Hezekiah prayed when the Assyrians marched on Jerusalem (previous chapter, 2 Kings 19). Jehoshaphat prayed when an alliance of foreign nations marched on Jerusalem (2 Chronicles 20).

It is worth noting that Jehoshaphat learned the value of prayer by watching his father Asa. The Bible describes Asa as a God-fearing king who, "did what was right in the eyes of the LORD his God." (2 Chronicles 14:2) Asa's accomplishments were numerous and promoted genuine worship in Israel (2 Chronicles 14:3-16). One noteworthy incident was the time Asa and Judah were attacked by a million man army from Ethiopia (2 Chronicles 14:9). Like a good king, Asa courageously led his outnumbered army to the field of battle (2 Chronicles 14:10). Like a godly king, Asa prayed a remarkable prayer to the LORD asking for deliverance (2 Chronicles 14:11). The LORD heard and answered Asa's prayer, and the Ethiopians were routed (2 Chronicles 14:12-15). All the while, young Jehoshaphat was watching his father, learning about the power of prayer.

In a strange way, the end of Asa's life continued to teach Jehoshaphat about the importance of prayer. The latter years of Asa's life were not marked by the humble obedience and consistent prayer that characterized his early years. In fact, 2 Chronicles 16:1-10 tell us that when the Northern Kingdom of Israel attacked the Southern Kingdom of Judah, Asa chose to rely on his allies in Syria instead of the LORD. Not long after this spiritual failure,

Asa again stumbled in his walk with God. The Bible explains Asa was diseased in his feet. Instead of praying to God for healing, Asa chose to trust doctors (2 Chronicles 16:12). Again, young Jehoshaphat was watching his father, learning from his spiritual failures. From the positive and negative example set by his father Asa, King Jehoshaphat learned to be a godly man of prayer.

We meet Jehoshaphat in 2 Chronicles 17:1-6. These verses tell us that Jehoshaphat strengthened the military power of Judah and encouraged Judah to worship the LORD. We also learn that Jehoshaphat was "courageous in the ways of the LORD." (2 Chronicles 17:6) This was the overall patter of Jehoshaphat the man and Jehoshaphat the king. He loved the LORD and encouraged Judah to be devoted to the LORD. But Jehoshaphat was not a perfect king. Despite his love for God, Jehoshaphat repeatedly made alliances with the wicked kings of Israel (Ahab in 2 Chronicles 18:1-19:3, Ahaziah in 2 Chronicles 20:35-37). His alliance with Ahab nearly cost him his life (2 Chronicles 18:31), and his alliance with Ahaziah cost him a fleet of ships (2 Chronicles 20:35-37).

So Jehoshaphat was not a perfect king. He made the mistake of aligning himself with scoundrels. But the overall story of his life is a man who loved God and strengthened Judah (2 Chronicles 17:1-6). Both of those characteristics were put to the test when a three-nation alliance marched on Jerusalem. The Bible tells us the Moabites and the Ammonites and the Meunites teamed up to destroy Jehoshaphat (2 Chronicles 20:1). While the size of this three-nation army is not quantified, it is described as "a great multitude." (2 Chronicles 20:2) When news of this three-nation-multitude reached the ears of godly king Jehoshaphat, the Bible demonstrates he was afraid (2 Chronicles 20:3).

Make no mistake about it. This was a turning point for the king of Judah. Option one, Jehoshaphat could trust in his alliance with the apostate Northern Kingdom of Israel. Option two, Jehoshaphat could follow the example of his father Asa and find security in an alliance with a foreign nation (see Asa's alliance with Syria above). Option three, Jehoshaphat could follow the example of his father Asa and turn to the LORD for deliverance (see Asa's battle with Ethiopia above).

As tempting as the first two options might have been, the Bible records Jehoshaphat, "set his face to seek the LORD." (2 Chronicles 20:3) Not only did Jehoshaphat personally turn to the LORD for help, but he also encouraged Israel to seek the LORD. The Bible records he, "proclaimed a fast throughout all Judah. And Judah assembled to seek help from the LORD." (2 Chronicles 20:3-4) Before getting to the actual prayer Jehoshaphat prayed, don't miss these lessons. Corporate prayer and fasting are important. Jehoshaphat led the people of Judah to give up food in order to seek help from the LORD and in order to seek the LORD himself (2 Chronicles 20:4). In other words, they fasted and prayed, not just because they wanted to be delivered from the multitude marching their direction. They also fasted and prayed to seek God himself. They didn't just want God's blessings. They also wanted God.

The prayer Jehoshaphat prayed is recorded in 2 Chronicles 20:5-12. Take a moment to read this prayer, and note the parts of Jehoshaphat's prayer. First, he focused the people on the truth about God (2 Chronicles 20:6-7). Second, he reminded the people of the certainty of God's promises (2 Chronicles 20:8-9). In looking back to God's promises, Jehoshaphat actually quoted part of the prayer Solomon prayed at the dedication of the temple (see chapter six, 1 Kings 8). Third, he acknowledged that Judah's situation was indeed dire (2 Chronicles 20:10-11). Finally, he ended with one of my favorite prayers in the Bible: "O our God, will you not execute judgment on them? For we are powerless against this great horde that is coming against us. We do not know what to do, but our eyes are on you." (2 Chronicles 20:12)

As the people listened to their king pray, God spoke to and through a prophet named Jahaziel who was in the congregation (2 Chronicles 20:14). Jahaziel told the people they need not be afraid. God wanted them to march out against the three nation army, hold their position, and watch the salvation of the LORD (2 Chronicles 20:15-17). Jehoshaphat and the people responded by first falling down in worship, and second standing to sing praise to God (2 Chronicles 20:18-19). Note that salvation had not yet come. The three nation army was still on the move. But the people trusted in the promises of God and responded with praise and worship.

Early the next morning the people arose and marched out into the wilderness (2 Chronicles 20:20). Again Jehoshaphat led the people. And again they offered praise and worship the LORD, trusting that God would be true to his word (2 Chronicles 20:20-21). The Bible demonstrates that as Jehoshaphat and the people sang to the LORD, the LORD responded by setting an ambush against the three nation army (2 Chronicles 20:22). First the Ammonites and Moabites destroyed the Meunites, then they turned and destroyed each other (2 Chronicles 20:22-23). When the people of Judah arrived at the battlefield they found mountains of dead bodies (2 Chronicles 20:24). The Bible demonstrates it took them three days to recover all the spoil, none of which they had to fight for (2 Chronicles 20:25). All of this came about because Jehoshaphat knew where to turn for help in the moment of crisis. He did not turn to Israel. He did not turn to Syria. He turned to the LORD, and he prayed for deliverance. Jehoshaphat put Psalm 50:15 into practice: "Call upon me in the day of trouble; I will deliver you, and you shall glorify me."

Three lessons are worth noting. First, future generations will learn from our example. At times Asa was faithful in prayer, like when he was attached by the million man army from Ethiopia. At other times Asa failed to pray, like when he was attacked by Israel and later when he was sick. This inconsistency in prayer was passed on to his son. Jehoshaphat prayed a remarkable prayer when he was attacked by this three nation army. At other times Jehoshaphat took comfort in his political alliance with Israel. The take away today is simple. Our example will teach the next generation about prayer. In large part, they will pray (or not pray) because of the example we set (or fail to set).

Second, it is ok to find yourself at a loss for words in prayer. Jehoshaphat reminded the people about the truth of God and his promises. He acknowledged the seriousness of their predicament. Then he just flat out admitted that they did not know what to do. They were stumped and they were powerless. If you've been in that kind of situation, don't be discouraged. Do what Jehoshaphat did. Fix your eyes on God. Wait. Watch.

Third, remember that in prayer, as we seek God's help, we also seek God himself (2 Chronicles 20:4). We do not come just for the gifts, but we also come for the Giver. Jehoshaphat and the people understood this, and it empowered them to respond to God in worship *before* they were saved from their enemies. They understood, and we must understand, that God is worthy of our praise, period, without condition. It does not matter how God responds to our prayers. It does not matter when God responds to our prayers. We bring our requests and our fears to God in prayer, and we walk away knowing that God is worthy of all the worship we can offer.

LEARNING TO PRAY

Ben collapsed into the chair on the other side of his pastor's desk. He couldn't even muster the strength to sit up straight, let alone hold a stiff upper lip. Instead, Ben slumped in the chair crying hysterically. His pastor had a pretty good idea of what was going on in Ben's life, but he also knew Ben needed to talk. Ben's pastor sat quietly while Ben unloaded the latest drama of his life.

First, his marriage with Carrie was still in shambles. Ben and Carrie had come to their pastor for counseling on several occasions. While the visits helped some, the relationship was far from healthy. Ben recalled the latest struggles to his pastor. Stories about miscommunication, disagreements about parenting, and arguments about money. No one had been unfaithful, but Ben and Carrie were not happy. No one was giving up, but Ben and Carrie were frustrated. Ben's pastor just listened.

Without any break in the conversation, Ben began talking about his teenage daughter Casey. She underperformed in school. She refused to do housework. She dated a guy Ben was less than enamored with. Then came the bombshell. Casey was pregnant, and the unimpressive boyfriend was the father. Ben didn't know what to do or how to advise his daughter. Should Casey get married? Should Ben punch the boyfriend? Should Ben let the unmarried couple move into his home? Should Ben try to make Casey finish school? Again, Ben's pastor just listened.

Without any break, Ben moved on to another area of frustration, work. Ben had worked for the same company since college, and he had done well for himself. He had received promotions and raises and more responsibility. The promotions and raises were nice. The responsibility had a downside. With the recession in full swing, Ben's company was scaling back. To make matters worse, Ben's boss wanted Ben to break the news to several members of his crew. Ben's job was not in jeopardy, but he hated to be the bearer of bad news. Again, Ben's pastor just listened.

Finally there was silence. Ben was done venting. After a full minute of quiet, he looked up and asked his pastor for advice. What should he do? How should be pray? Where should he turn? Ben's pastor knew this was no time for platitudes and greeting card advice. This was no time deliver a theological lesson on the sovereignty of God in all situations and circumstances. Instead of advice, Ben's pastor told Ben to go home and read 2 Chronicles 20. In this chapter Ben read about a man named Jehoshaphat who came to the end of his rope. He had nowhere to turn. He did not know what to do. So he prayed. The funny thing is, Jehoshaphat didn't even know what to pray. He simply admitted that he didn't know what to do, and he told God he was looking to him for help. That's it. That's what he prayed. And that's what Ben prayed. He didn't need anyone to assure him everything would be ok. He did need to fix his eyes on God in the midst of chaos and crisis. He needed to pray, and this was a start.

QUESTIONS FOR DISCUSSION

1. What have people taught you to pray, either through positive or negative examples? What have you learned about prayer from others? Who are you teaching to pray?

2. When you don't know what to pray, how does looking to God in faith change you?

3. In prayer, are you seeking God himself, or are you simply seeking God's gifts?

CHAPTER 10

EZRA PRAYS FOR SAFETY

For I was ashamed to ask the king for a band of
soldiers and horsemen to protect us against the
enemy on our way. (Ezra 8:22)

THE APOSTATE NORTHERN KINGDOM OF ISRAEL WAS
defeated by Assyria and sent into exile in 722 BC (2 Kings
17:6-23). Over one hundred years later, in approximately
587 BC, the Southern Kingdom of Judah was defeated by
Babylon and sent into exile (2 Kings 25:1-21). This was
the low point for God's chosen people. They had come
through the wilderness wanderings. They had endured
the dark days of the judges. They experienced the horror of civil war. But this was the low point. The chosen
people of God had been defeated and sent into exile in
foreign lands. The holy city of Jerusalem and the great
temple were distant memories for the exiles in Assyria
and Babylon. They had been forcibly removed from the

land God had promised to Abraham and Isaac and Jacob. They were far from home because their hearts had been far from God. It would be decades before any of them would be allowed to return to the Promised Land.

In 538 BC, the first wave of exiles returned with a man named Zerubbabel (Ezra 2). They were sent by Cyrus king of Persia, and they were sent to rebuild Yahweh's temple in Jerusalem. Eighty years later, in 458 BC, a second wave of exiles returned with a man named Ezra (Ezra 7-8). Unlike Zerubbabel, Ezra's job required no physical construction. Ezra was sent to train leaders by teaching the Law of Moses to the exiles who had previously returned to the land (Ezra 7:25). In other words, Ezra was sent to teach and preach the Bible to God's people. A third wave of exiles returned in 444 BC with a man named Nehemiah (Nehemiah 1-2). Their mission was rebuilding the walls of Jerusalem.

Ezra is our focus, and we meet him for the first time in chapter 7 of the book that bears his name. We learn that Ezra was a descendant of Aaron the high priest and brother of Moses (Ezra 7:1-5). We learn that he had been exiled to Babylon (Ezra 7:6). We learn that he was a scribe skilled in the Law of Moses, meaning he knew the Scriptures (Ezra 7:6). We learn that Ezra had, "set his heart to study the Law of the LORD, and to do it and to teach his statutes and rules in Israel." (Ezra 7:10) Maybe most importantly, we learn the secret to Ezra's success. The Bible records the hand of God was with Ezra, and as a result he found favor in the eyes of King Artaxerxes (Ezra 7:6, 9).

This favor included a special letter Ezra received from Artaxerxes (Ezra 7:11). Because Ezra had a letter from the king, he was allowed to take anyone who wanted to return to Jerusalem, he carried treasure given to him by the king, he had permission to buy sacrifices and supplies in Jerusalem, and he was granted permission to use any extra money at his discretion (Ezra 7:12-24).

With the hand of God upon him, and the favor of Artaxerxes supporting him, Ezra set off with a motley group of peasants, priests, Levites, singers, gatekeepers, and temple servants (Ezra 7:7). Noticeably absent from this list is any mention of soldiers or warriors or guards or body builders or tough guys or ninjas or Marines. Ezra was leading a group of peasants and pastors on a long journey, and they were carrying a small fortune. What about highway robbers? What about bandits? What about thieves? What about militias? Ezra had no recourse but to trust God for protection. And Ezra knew he had good reason to trust God for protection. He was confident that God had worked on the heart of Artaxerxes (Ezra 7:27), and he took courage knowing that God was with him (Ezra 7:28).

That's where Ezra 7 leaves off, with Ezra taking courage in the LORD. Then in Ezra 8 we read about Ezra's travel preparation. He listed the people traveling with him

(Ezra 8:1-14). He camped out with the group for three days beside the Ahava River (Ezra 8:15). He invited a group of Levites to make the trip (Ezra 8:16-20). And somewhere in the midst of all these preparations, reality hit Ezra like a Mack truck. He was leading a group of peasants and pastors on a long journey, and they were carrying a small fortune!

Ezra had several options. Option one, he could give into fear and call the whole trip off. The downside to this was obvious. God's hand was upon him, God had directed the heart of Artaxerxes, and God wanted Ezra to return and teach the Bible to the people. Option two, he could ask Artaxerxes for an armed escort. Again, the downside to this option was obvious. In Ezra 8:22 we read that Ezra was ashamed to ask for the armed escort because he had previously told Artaxerxes, "The hand of our God is for good on all who seek him, and the power of his wrath is against all who forsake him." If Ezra turned around and asked for an armed escort to Israel, the God of Israel would look impotent.

This left Ezra with only one real option: prayer. Ezra 8:21-23 describes Ezra leading his rag-tag group of exiles in a pre-trip prayer meeting. This prayer meeting was a corporate event. It was more than individuals praying for the same thing. It was individuals praying together for the same thing. So many of the great prayers in the Bible are corporate events where God's people gathered together to join their hearts in prayer. Most modern day

Wednesday night prayer meetings deserve their fair share of ridicule. However, believers who laugh at the idea of a Wednesday night prayer meeting ought to look long and hard at the Bible prayers that involved God's people praying together.

Ezra's prayer in Ezra 8:21-23 also involved fasting and humility. Not only did the people abstain from food, they did it on the verge of a long, arduous journey from Babylon to Jerusalem. This fast was designed to focus their hearts on God and the specific request they were bringing before God. And as they fasted, Ezra writes they humbled themselves before God. In other words, they did not come to God with the idea that their praying somehow put God at their beck-and-call. God was under absolutely no obligation to hear their prayer or grant their request. As a man who knew God's Word, Ezra was aware of these realities, and he led the people to humble themselves before their God.

The specific request of Ezra's prayer in Ezra 8:21-23 was quite simple. Ezra and the people implored God and asked him for, "a safe journey for ourselves, our children, and all our goods." (Ezra 8:22) Lest anyone think this request was selfish in nature, remember these exiles were poor peasants who had lost everything a few decades earlier. They were not traveling with name brand clothing and designer furniture. These exiles travelled with the clothes on their back, their families, and a small fortune given to them by Artaxerxes. Also remember that the "goods" mentioned in verse 22 were the money and supplies Artaxerxes sent with Ezra for temple worship. This fortune was to be used for the beautification of the temple and worship in Jerusalem (Ezra 7:15-24). It was these "goods" that Ezra and the people prayed about, asking God for a safe journey.

In Ezra 8:23 we learn that God heard the entreaty of the people. That was good news, but it was not the end of the matter. The journey still had to be made, and the dangers were still very real. Ezra 8:24 describes Ezra taking wise action by dividing the treasure among the Levites. I believe Ezra was thinking strategically here (see Jacob's strategy in Genesis 32:8). Should bandits attack the group, the treasure would be divided and some of the Levites may be able to escape. The lesson in Ezra's action is an important one. Prayer is powerful and should always be our first response to a crisis. However, there is no reason to take unnecessary risks or to act foolishly simply because we have "bathed" a matter in prayer. God wants us to pray. He also wants us to use our brains. Ezra did both by praying and then dividing the treasure among the Levites.

After the three day corporate prayer meeting, and after Ezra's wise and strategic action, the people set off on their journey (Ezra 8:31). The Bible demonstrates, "The hand of our God was on us, and he delivered us from the hand of the enemy and from ambushes by the way." (Ezra 8:31)

One wonders what this deliverance looked like. Was it miraculous? Were angelic warriors involved? Did the LORD strike down the enemy in spectacular fashion? Or was the deliverance ordinary and mundane and boring? We are left to wonder about some of the specifics, but one thing is clear. Ezra and the people prayed for a safe journey. God heard their prayer. And everyone arrived safely with all the treasure in Jerusalem (Ezra 8:32-34).

Learning to Pray

Cody is the missions pastor at his church. His job involves establishing partnerships with missionaries and churches, balancing local and foreign missions, and planning and leading mission teams from his church. Sometimes Cody wishes he could be overseas on the mission field all the time. But Cody also loves seeing the members of his church become engaged in the Great Commission.

One thing Cody does not enjoy about his job is the occasional critic of foreign missions. He tries to be patient, and he tries to listen to people express their concerns. But sometimes the objections make him want to scream. Some people talk about the importance of taking care of local missions before global missions. Cody believes in the necessity of local missions, but he also knows that needs at home do not absolve his church of the responsibility to take the gospel to the ends of the earth. Other people talk about the danger of leaving the United States.

Cody knows the world is a dangerous place, but he also knows there are plenty of dangers in his own backyard.

Despite these objections to global missions, Cody presses on with the mission of making disciples of all nations. He continues to look for ways to plug people into the mission, and he is excited about the trip he will lead this summer. There's only one problem. Even as Cody stands before his church to rally the troops to action, he has several nagging fears in the back of his mind. For one thing, in recent months several commercial flights just vanished over the ocean. Cody knows the statistics on air travel, but when you are leading a team you can't help but worry. Another nagging fear is terrorism. Just this week he read about an attack in Western Europe that left a dozen dead. Cody knows the summer team is headed to a part of the world that is far more dangerous than Western Europe. Add to this the worldwide Ebola hysteria. Cody knows his team will be thousands of miles away from the hot spots, but what about planes and airports?

When he finds himself worrying about these issues, Cody does two things. First, he reminds himself that the Great Commission does not have an exemption clause for plane crashes, terrorism, or disease. He knows risk is right when it involves taking the gospel to those who have never heard the name of Jesus. So first, Cody preaches to himself, reminding himself of the urgency and necessity of global missions.

Second, Cody prays. In recent years, he has found the prayer of Ezra in Ezra 8 to be particularly helpful. Ezra and the exiles traveling with him prayed together for a safe journey. It was corporate prayer. Cody encourages his church and the mission team to pray individually. But he also looks for opportunities for his church and the mission team to pray together on a regular basis. Ezra and the exiles fasted as they prayed. Again, Cody looks for opportunities to encourage individual and corporate fasting in preparation for the trip. Cody leads his team from prayer to courageous action. He leads by example, refusing to let fear paralyze the mission. Like Ezra, he knows that his team is engaging in a God-ordained mission. The dangers and the risks are real, but the mission is worth it. Cody prays for his team. Cody prays with his team. Then Cody leads the team to boldly proclaim the name of Jesus.

Questions for Discussion

1. Does Ezra's prayer change the way you pray for safe travel? If so, how?

2. How has corporate prayer impacted your life? How can you give more time to corporate prayer?

3. How does fasting play out in your personal prayer life, if at all? How should fasting impact your prayer life?

CHAPTER 11

NEHEMIAH PRAYS WITHOUT CEASING

Remember me, O my God, for good. (Nehemiah 13:31)

IN 1 THESSALONIANS 5:17 THE APOSTLE PAUL WRITES IT IS God's will for all believers to "pray without ceasing." This is one of the best known Bible passages about prayer. It's also one of the most misapplied Bible passages about prayer. Usually this verse comes up when someone has been put on the spot about their prayer life. The conversation goes something like this: "How often do I pray? How much time to I spend in prayer? Well, I agree with Paul. I try to pray without ceasing. A regular, dedicated prayer time doesn't work well for my schedule. So I just try to pray constantly throughout the day." What they really mean is this: "I haven't prayed in four months."

1 Thessalonians 5:17 is not an exemption clause that gives us permission to neglect a regular, consistent, dedicated prayer life. At the same time, there is something to the idea that we should be people who pray frequently, throughout the day, about all sorts of things. So on the one hand we should set aside time specifically for prayer. And on the other hand we should pray spontaneously throughout the day. One of the best examples of this balance is Nehemiah.

Nehemiah lived several hundred years before Jesus, and he was involved in the exiles returning from Babylon to Jerusalem. Zerubbabel led the first wave of returning exiles in 538 BC (Ezra 2). His mission was rebuilding the temple in Jerusalem. Ezra led the second wave of returning exiles in 458 BC (Ezra 7-8). His mission was teaching the Law of God. Nehemiah led the third wave of returning exiles in 444 BC (Nehemiah 1-2). His mission was rebuilding the ruined walls of Jerusalem. From the first chapter of Nehemiah to the final words of Nehemiah 13:31, we see a man who prayed without ceasing.

What we know of Nehemiah's prayer life begins in Nehemiah 1:1-3. While in exile, Nehemiah received word that despite the progress made by Zerubbabel and Ezra, the walls of Jerusalem were still in ruins. Upon hearing this news, Nehemiah sat down and wept and mourned and fasted and prayed for days (Nehemiah 1:4). One of the prayers he prayed during this time is recorded in Nehemiah 1:5-11. Take a few minutes to read this remarkable prayer, and note the following lessons about prayer.

First, this prayer flowed out of a regular, dedicated, intentional prayer time. This was not prayer on the run. This was not prayer during your commute. This was not prayer while you exercise. This was Nehemiah stopping his daily activities to devote a significant amount of time to prayer. In following chapters of Nehemiah we see a man who does pray spontaneously about all sorts of things. But understand that part of praying without ceasing does involve regular, dedicated, intentional prayer time.

Second, this prayer begins with God. Nehemiah's first words are an acknowledgement that the LORD is God of heaven who keeps his covenants (Nehemiah 1:5). After acknowledging the LORD as God, Nehemiah humbly asks God to listen to his request (Nehemiah 1:6). All good prayers should center on God. Whether the first words or the last words or the middle words acknowledge God as God, good prayers center on God.

Third, Nehemiah confesses corporate and family and personal sin (Nehemiah 1:6-7). This is surprising because immediately before he confessed sin, Nehemiah asked God to hear his request. One expects the actual request to follow. Instead, Nehemiah launches into confession, admitting that Israel and his family and he himself had sinned. He does not make excuses. He does not try to explain their shortcomings. He does not blame his environment or his circumstances. He just admits, "We have acted very corruptly against you and have not kept the commandments, the statues, and the rules that you commanded your servant Moses." (Nehemiah 1:7) Confession does not have to be part of every prayer, but confession is part of praying without ceasing.

Fourth, Nehemiah asks God to remember his covenant promises (Nehemiah 1:8-10). He freely acknowledges that God warned his people through Moses about the consequences of unfaithfulness (Nehemiah 1:8). But he also trusts in the promises of God to forgive when his people repent (Nehemiah 1:9). Nehemiah ends this part of his prayer by reminding God that Israel was his nation, his people (Nehemiah 1:10). Yes they deserved exile from the land, but the reputation of God was at stake in the future of his people. In all of these prayers, Nehemiah is praying the Bible back to God. He is basing his prayers of prior revelation. He is listening to Scripture and responding in faith. This reminds us that part of praying without ceasing is consistent Bible intake. We cannot pray without ceasing unless we are hearing from God through his Word on a regular basis.

Finally, Nehemiah again asks God to hear his request (Nehemiah 1:11). The actual request was simple: "Give success to your servant today, and grant him mercy in the sight of this man." (Nehemiah 1:11) The "servant" was Nehemiah, and the "man" was King Artaxerxes.

Apparently Nehemiah was a high ranking official in Artaxerxes administration (Nehemiah 1:11). When Nehemiah learned about the still ruined walls of Jerusalem, he decided to call in a favor with his boss. He planned to ask Artaxerxes for permission to return home and rebuild the walls of Jerusalem. But before asking the king for a personal favor, Nehemiah prayed. He prayed for days (Nehemiah 1:4). He prayed a humble prayer that centered on God and was based on God's Word (Nehemiah 1:5-11). He prayed, asking God to give him favor in the eyes of Artaxerxes (Nehemiah 1:11).

Nehemiah 2:1-8 describes Nehemiah asking Artaxerxes for permission to return to Jerusalem and rebuild the walls. Interestingly, in Nehemiah 2:4, just before Nehemiah actually asked Artaxerxes for his blessing, we read that Nehemiah prayed. It was probably a brief, silent prayer, but it was prayer without ceasing. Upon hearing Nehemiah's request, Artaxerxes agreed to the plan (Nehemiah 1:8). The Bible tells us that his agreement was due to the fact that the good hand of God was upon Nehemiah the prayer-warrior (Nehemiah 1:8).

The rest of the book of Nehemiah describes Nehemiah's return to Jerusalem as well as the work he organized. Eventually the walls of Jerusalem were repaired, but there were plenty of challenges and setbacks along the way. Through it all Nehemiah proved to be a man of prayer, a man who prayed without ceasing. The following list details the impromptu, spontaneous prayers of Nehemiah (and a few prayers of others).

- Nehemiah 4:4-5, Nehemiah prayed in response to the taunts of the enemy

- Nehemiah 4:9, Nehemiah prayed as they set a guard over their work

- Nehemiah 5:13, Nehemiah prayed judgment on anyone who broke the oath about not charging excessive interest on fellow Jews

- Nehemiah 5:19, Nehemiah prayed that God would remember his good work

- Nehemiah 6:9, Nehemiah prayed for strength when others lied about him

- Nehemiah 6:14, Nehemiah prayed that God would remember the sins of Tobiah and Sanballat as they tried to frighten the people

- Nehemiah 8:6, Ezra prayed a benediction as the people gathered to worship

- Nehemiah 9:1-38, the Levites prayed an extended and detailed prayer of confession as the people were gathered together for corporate repentance

- Nehemiah 12:27-43, Nehemiah prayed to dedicate the completed walls

- Nehemiah 13:14, 22, 29, Nehemiah prayed that God would remember him for confronting the people about their disobedience on various issues

- Nehemiah 13:31, Nehemiah prayed a final prayer that God would remember him for good

Prayer is a major part of the book of Nehemiah because prayer was a major part of Nehemiah's life. This was a man who prayed without ceasing. At times he devoted days specifically for prayer. At other times he offered one sentence, impromptu prayers. At times he prayed alone, silently. At other times he gathered with others for corporate prayer. At times he openly confessed his sin. At other times he asked God to remember his good deeds. Through all of it, Nehemiah prayed, and he prayed without ceasing.

LEARNING TO PRAY

Jenny's life was busy. It was her senior year of high school. On top of her classwork, Jenny was juggling basketball, student council, and college applications. After school she worked as a nanny. This job required her to haul kiddos all over town, clean house, and make trips to the grocery store. On top of school and work, Jenny did her best to be involved at church. She sang with the youth praise team each Wednesday night, which also meant she had to be at praise team practice each Sunday. Life was a whirlwind!

Jenny knew leaving town would force her to play catch up, but she never missed a youth trip. Also, since this was her senior year, she knew she didn't want to miss her last winter retreat to south Texas. The trip was like many she had been on over the last seven years. The bus ride was long. The camp food was gross. The bunks were hard. But the time spent with friends and the time spent in worship were phenomenal. This particular retreat focused on spiritual disciplines. Despite her busy life, Jenny did a remarkable job of reading her Bible and praying most days. This year she had set two goals. Read through the entire Bible and keep a prayer journal. All in all, the speaker did a good job of encouraging the students to practice spiritual disciplines, and Jenny returned home with several good suggestions.

One suggestion involved praying without ceasing. On Saturday night the camp pastor talked about Nehemiah. He walked the students through the book of Nehemiah showing them how Nehemiah the man prayed constantly. He prayed about good things and bad things, he prayed alone and with others, he prayed for his work and God's blessing. He prayed without ceasing!

Jenny realized her prayer life was far different than Nehemiah's. She realized that while she did a good job of maintaining a regular prayer time most mornings, she had a tendency to put her life on auto pilot as soon as she closed her Bible and prayer journal. Yes she prayed each morning, but her days were not filled with a spirit of prayer. On the ride home, Jenny resolved to do better at praying without ceasing.

Two weeks later, as she read back through her prayer journal, Jenny realized she had quickly gone back to her old ways. Her life was busy, and her morning prayer time was usually the last time she thought about anything spiritual until she woke up the next morning. This time she decided to do more than make a resolution. Jenny set an alarm on her phone. Every hour on the hour she would remind herself to pray throughout the day. The alarm went off at school, in traffic, during church, and while Jenny was watching TV. Whenever the alarm went off, Jenny found something to pray about. She wasn't where she wanted to be on the issue of prayer, but she was taking concrete steps to become a woman who prayed without ceasing.

QUESTIONS FOR DISCUSSION

1. What is harder for you: dedicated prayer time or spontaneous prayer? Why?

2. Do your prayers center on God or on your requests? How can you be more like Nehemiah on this issue?

3. Specifically and personally, what daily situations should drive you to pray?

Chapter 12

Asaph Prays through Doubt

Whom have I in heaven but you? And there is nothing on earth that I desire besides you. (Psalm 73:25)

Psalm 73 is one of my favorite passages in the Bible. I like this passage because it's honest, it's raw, and it deals with something we all experience in life: doubt. That may not sound spiritual. That may not sound mature. But let's all admit we struggle with doubt. Why did my family member get sick and die? Am I really a Christian? Am I actually doing anything significant with my life? Is the Bible and Christianity and Jesus and all of it really true? At some point in your life, you've probably struggled with doubt.

Psalm 73 is about the doubt of a man named Asaph. Even if you grew up in church, I'd be willing to bet you don't know much about Asaph. This is unfortunate, because even though Asaph doesn't play a major role in the story line of the Old Testament, he was a remarkable man of God. The Bible reveals Asaph was a member of the priestly tribe of Levi (1 Chronicles 6:39-47). He was involved in leading worship at the tabernacle, and his instrument of choice was the cymbals (1 Chronicles 6:31-32, 15:19, 16:4-5). Asaph was not just a musician, he was also a teacher who prophesied under the direction of David (1 Chronicles 25:1-2). He fathered a family of singers who served the LORD (Nehemiah 7:6-7, 44). In later years, after Asaph was dead and gone, he was remembered as a man of worship, faith, and obedience (Nehemiah 12:46, 2 Chronicles 20:13-17, 29:12-19). In addition to all this, Asaph was the author of numerous psalms (Psalm 50, 73-83).

The big picture of Asaph is clear. He was a big deal. He wasn't the kind of guy who thinks he's a big deal, but everyone else thinks he's a joke. Asaph really was a big deal. He could accurately be described as a spiritual giant. In fact, Nehemiah 12:46 looks back in time and refers to "the days of David and Asaph." That would be like someone in 100 years saying, "Hey, remember back in 2014, back in the days of [insert name of famous politician or celebrity or athlete] and [insert your name]." Nehemiah looked back on the good old days of Israel and said, "Remember the days of David and Asaph."

Asaph was a big deal. He was a spiritual giant. He was a leader in Israel. And he struggled with doubt. Asaph looked around and he noticed that the wicked seemed to be doing fine. In fact, the wicked seemed to be doing better than the righteous. This disparity threw Asaph's faith into turmoil. He was angry with God. He questioned God. He doubted God. He wanted to know why the righteous struggled to make ends meet while the wicked prospered. He also wanted to know why God didn't do something to change this situation. Psalm 73 is the story of how these doubts played out in his prayer life.

Take a moment to read Psalm 73, verse 1 all the way to verse 28. This psalm can be broken down into five sections. Section one, "truth" (Psalm 73:1). Section two, "confusion" (Psalm 73:2-15). Section three, "truth" (Psalm 73:16-20). Section four, "confession" (Psalm 73:21-22). Section five, "truth" (Psalm 73:23-28). Based on this outline, the big idea is obvious. It's OK to struggle with doubts. It's even OK to question God. But you must begin with the truth, center on the truth, and end with the truth.

Asaph began with truth. Specifically, he began by preaching the truth to himself. Before he ever brought a doubt or question or objection before God, he confessed, "Truly God is good to Israel, to those who are pure in heart." (Psalm 73:1) This was a truth that did not seem true in Asaph's situation. It was a truth that did not seem to fit with real life. But it was truth. And before Asaph wallowed in his doubts, he preached the truth to himself.

Believers have three enemies who constantly preach lies. The world preaches, telling us we need money and possessions to be satisfied. Our flesh preaches, telling us sin will bring more pleasure than a clean conscience. The devil himself preaches, telling us that God doesn't care about our issues and problems. Day in and day out, lies are constantly being preached to the heart of every believer. Your pastor gets thirty minutes a week. Your Sunday school teacher gets another thirty minutes. The rest of the week it's a steady stream of lies from the world, your flesh, and the devil. This is why you must preach the truth to yourself. The godly men and women in the Bible understood this, and that's why so much of their prayers are simply statements of what is true about God.

After Asaph began with the truth, he moved on to confusion. In Psalm 73:2-15 Asaph had his eyes on the wrong things. At times, he focused on the wicked and their prosperity (Psalm 73:2-12). At other times, he focused on himself and his ability to make sense of life's problems (Psalm 73:13-15). Because his focus is in the wrong place, because Asaph allowed his doubts to dominate, he actually started to think his relationship with God was a waste of time (Psalm 73:13). Two verses later, Asaph admitted that this thought was not something he verbalized in prayer (Psalm 73:15). Instead, Asaph refrained from making this blasphemous comment, and he kept his thoughts to himself.

There is an important lesson about prayer in these verses. All Bible believing Christians understand that God knows the thoughts of our heart before they ever roll off our tongue. You've probably heard someone say something like, "If you're thinking it, you might as well say it, because God already knows it." While there is truth to that sentiment, there is also wisdom in restraint. As Asaph pondered his doubts and questions and frustrations, he refrained from making blasphemous statements to God in prayer. Did God know he was thinking these things? Absolutely! At the same time, was it right for Asaph to keep his mouth shut? Absolutely! Some thoughts do not need to be verbalized in prayer, and Asaph was right to keep this thought to himself.

The third section of Psalm 73 involves more truth. In Psalm 73:16-20 Asaph refocused his heart on God through worship. He went to the sanctuary of God, humbling himself before the LORD in worship (Psalm 73:17). When Asaph fixed his eyes on the LORD, he began to see the world more clearly (Psalm 73:18-20). I hope you see the importance of worship. I hope you see the value of setting aside time each day to refocus your heart on the truth about God. I hope you see the value of setting aside time each week to gather with other believers a refocus your heart on the truth about God. Without this time of worship, your doubts and questions and frustrations will go unchecked. With this time of worship, your focus is realigned and you see the problems of life more clearly.

Worship led Asaph to confession. When he saw God clearly, he also saw himself clearly. His response was a prayer of confession. Without making excuses for his folly, Asaph simply confessed that when he doubted and questioned the goodness of God, he acted like a beast, and he spoke out of his ignorance (Psalm 73:21-22). If you commit yourself to regular worship, this sort of prayer will be part of your prayer life. Focusing on the truth of God has a funny way of revealing the truth about ourselves. When we see ourselves as we are, the only fitting response is a prayer of confession.

Finally, Asaph ended with truth. The prayer of Psalm 73:23-28 contains some of the most beautiful words found in the Bible. Asaph acknowledged that God was continually with him, constantly upholding him, always guiding him (Psalm 73:23-24). Asaph declared that the only joy of heaven that appealed to him was God himself (Psalm 73:25). Asaph declared that there was nothing on earth he desired more than God (Psalm 73:25). Asaph recognized God as his sustainer and his strength (Psalm 73:26). Asaph ended by coming full circle. Previously he questioned the usefulness of his faith. Now he insists that it is "good to be near God." (Psalm 73:28). He even pledges to tell others about the goodness of God and the glory of his works (Psalm 73:28).

Psalm 73 is the prayer of a godly man who struggled with doubt. It's also a pattern to follow when doubts and questions assail our faith. Is it OK to be honest with

God? Certainly, but some thoughts are better left unsaid. Rather than rant and rave against our Creator like an ignorant beast, we must preach the truth to ourselves, and we must focus our hearts on God through worship. When we do this we will join Asaph in seeing God as infinitely beautiful and glorious. When you see God in this way, prayer becomes easy.

Learning to Pray

Craig grew up in a Christian family, attended church regularly, and was baptized in middle school. All through high school he called himself a Christian. Now Craig was a junior in college and things were different. He only went to church when he went home and stayed with his parents. He never read the Bible and seldom prayed. Craig couldn't tell you exactly when he stopped believing in Jesus, but somewhere in his college experience his faith seemed to fade away.

Maybe the death of his younger brother had something to do with his slide from faith. Brandon was three years younger than Craig. During Craig's first year in college Brandon died in a car accident. A drunk driver crossed over the median and hit Craig's car. The whole thing seemed so senseless, and Craig struggled to feel God's presence in the months after the accident.

In addition to Brandon's death, Craig felt as if a whole new world had been opened to him at college. It seemed that every class and every professor gave Craig a new reason to question his faith. His biology and chemistry professors talked about evolution with confidence. His history professor talked about the historical inaccuracies in the Bible. His psychology professor explained everything with no reference to God. His philosophy professor traced the historical development of powerful ideas, most of which had nothing to do with the Bible. Craig wondered why his parents or his youth pastor had never talked about the questions he was dealing with at college.

When Craig needed one more elective course to fill his schedule, New Testament seemed like an unlikely candidate. However, the class fit well with his schedule, and Craig had heard good things about the professor. On the first day of class, the professor encouraged the students to approach the New Testament with an open mind. He also encouraged the students to find a church. He didn't push one denomination over another, but he encouraged the students to be involved in a church during their semester of New Testament study. For some strange reason, Craig decided to accept his professor's challenge. He found a church nearby and began attending on Sundays.

As the semester wore on, something unexpected happened in Craig's life. He found himself believing despite his doubts. Was it the New Testament class? Was it his new church? Craig wasn't exactly certain. What he did know was the despite his previous doubts (many of which still remained), he once again found himself drawn to Jesus. When the pastor preached on Psalm 73 Craig connected the dots. Asaph had spiritual doubts just like Craig, and the doubts were only erased when he committed himself to worship. Craig found the prayer of Psalm 73 fitting in his own life. He appreciated the honesty of Asaph's questions. He was challenged by his humble repentance. And he committed to pray the beautiful words of praise at the end of the psalm.

QUESTIONS FOR DISCUSSION

1. In your prayer life, how can you begin with the truth, center on the truth, and end with the truth?

2. How much of your prayer life involves statements that are true of God?

3. How does personal and corporate worship provide a check against your doubts?

CHAPTER 13

AGUR PRAYS A MODEL PRAYER

Remove far from me falsehood and lying; give me
neither poverty nor riches. (Proverbs 30:8)

PEOPLE LOVE THE BOOK OF PROVERBS. MAYBE BECAUSE
Proverbs is direct and to the point. Maybe because Proverbs is so easy to apply to everyday life. Maybe because
Proverbs fits well with our pragmatism. Maybe because
Proverbs is conveniently divided into a monthly reading
program. Maybe because Proverbs is the one book of the
Bible you can actually open up and read a verse with no
context and still make sense of the verse. For all these
reasons and more, people love the book of Proverbs.

Traditionally, Proverbs is attributed to Solomon. While
a majority of the book is connected with the wise king
of Israel, there are actually four collections of proverbs

within the book of Proverbs. Chapters 1-24 are designated as proverbs of Solomon. Chapters 25-29 contain this note, "These also are proverbs of Solomon which the men of Hezekiah king of Judah copied." So Solomon wrote these proverbs, but the content was edited and arranged by the scribes of King Hezekiah. Chapter 30 bears the name of Agur son of Jakeh, and chapter 31 bears the name of King Lemuel. Taken in order the four divisions of Proverbs are attributed to Solomon, Solomon through Hezekiah's scribes, Agur, and Lemuel.

The topics covered in Proverbs vary, sometimes chapter to chapter, sometimes verse to verse. Prayer is not a major theme in Proverbs. However, prayer is mentioned throughout the book, and the lessons offered are invaluable. For example, Proverbs 1:20-33 explains that God is not amused with "get-me-out-of-trouble" prayers offered by those who persistently and consistently walk in sin. Proverbs 2:1-5 promises that if you pray for wisdom and you keep God's commandments, God will give you wisdom. Proverbs 15:8 and 29 assure us that God accepts the prayer of the "upright." Proverbs 21:13 explains that our relationship with other people has an impact on our prayer life. Proverbs 28:9 warns that God will have no regard for the prayers of people who have no regard for his law. Proverbs 28:13 offers hope by telling us that confession and repentance lead to God's mercy.

In all these important passages about prayer, the one thing that is missing is prayer itself! In fact, there is only one prayer in the entire book of Proverbs, and it is not a prayer prayed by Solomon. In Proverbs 30:7-9 we read about a most interesting prayer prayed by Agur son of Jakeh. Here is what this unknown wise man prayed, "Two things I ask of you; deny them not to me before I die: Remove far from me falsehood and lying; give me neither poverty nor riches; feed me with the food that is needful for me, lest I be full and deny you and say, 'Who is the LORD?' or lest I be poor and steal and profane the name of my God." (Proverbs 30:7-9)

Like the rest of Proverbs, Agur's prayer is simple and straightforward. He comes with two requests. First, Agur asks God to remove "falsehood" and "lying" from his life. Second, Agur asks God to meet his needs without making him too rich or too poor. Then comes his rational. Agur knows his heart. He knows that if he is "full" and wealthy, he will be tempted to take credit for his prosperity and deny the work of God. He also knows that if he is "poor" and needy, he will be tempted to take matters into his own hands by stealing instead of trusting God to provide. This brings Agur's prayer full circle. Whatever his lot in life, he does not want to "deny" the LORD, and he does not want to "profane" God's name. So, he makes two simple requests. Request one, remove sin from my life. Request two, meet my needs without abundance or lack.

When I read Agur's prayer, I can't help but think of a popular book about prayer. In 2000 Bruce Wilkinson wrote *The Prayer of Jabez: Breaking Through to the Blessed Life.* By all accounts, the book was a commercial success. It was also a polarizing piece of Christian writing. Some hailed the book as the ultimate key to praying God's blessing into your life. Others criticized the book as nothing but health and wealth rubbish. Personally, I don't believe *The Prayer of Jabez* is as good as some say, nor do I believe it is as bad as others say. I do think the book presents a picture of prayer that is too automatic, and almost magical. There is a hint of animism in the idea that praying a specific formula will result in automatic results. However, I do not think Wilkinson is advocating a health and wealth gospel. He clearly warns his reader against assuming that God's blessing always means financial increase.

What many readers have taken away from *The Prayer of Jabez* is the idea that "increase" is somehow the key to God's blessing being poured into your life. We pray for increase, and God responds with blessing. Truth be told, there may be something right in this idea. Jabez is singled out for his character and his prayer. He is presented as a godly man who had suffered much (1 Chronicles 4:9). He is described as a man who prayed for God to "enlarge" his border (1 Chronicles 4:10). And in the end, we are simply told, "And God granted what he asked." (1 Chronicles 4:10).

So to be clear, no one is suggesting that we cut Jabez and 1 Chronicles 4:9-10 out of our Bibles. What might be needed, however, is balance. Especially in the United States, where we are so easily intrigued with the idea of "increase" and "enlarging our borders," we need balance. And if balance is what we need, Agur's prayer in Proverbs 30 is just the passage to level our sights. Agur never prayed for increase. He never asked for his borders or his influence or his bank account to be enlarged. Instead, Agur asked that God would meet his needs (Proverbs 30:8). More than that, he asked God not to make him too poor or too rich (Proverbs 30:8). In all of this, Agur was motivated by a desire to honor the LORD and bring glory to God's name (Proverbs 30:9). Agur simply wanted God to meet his needs while also removing the sin in his life (Proverbs 30:8).

Millions prayed the prayer of Jabez. Are you willing to pray the prayer of Agur? If you are, it goes something like this: "God, remove the sin in my life and give me a heart to love you more than anything this world has to offer. Don't make me rich because I don't want to trust in riches. Don't make me poor because I don't want to doubt your provision. If I deny your blessings or steal to meet my needs, I will bring shame upon myself and you. Ultimately I just want to bring glory to you. I trust you completely."

LEARNING TO PRAY

Casey and Jeff had been coworkers for eight years. Casey was in management, and Jeff ran a forklift in the warehouse. Somehow, despite having separate realms of responsibility, the two became friends. They often ate

135

lunch together and discussed things like sports, family, and even faith. Casey and Jeff did not attend the same church, but they were both faithful followers of Jesus. During their lunch discussions they enjoyed talking about what they were learning at their respective churches.

One spring day Casey was telling Jeff about the cruise his family was planning for the summer. As he talked about the various ports of call and all-you-can-eat food, Casey had an idea. They should go together! Jeff and his family should go on the same cruise! There kids were about the same age, and Casey was sure the two families would have a blast. Jeff was less than enthusiastic. Instead of giving any kind of answer, he tried to change the subject. When Casey pressed the issue, Jeff explained that his family could never afford the kind of vacation Casey was talking about. Lunch ended on an awkward note.

To be honest, Casey was shocked. He knew Jeff didn't make management money, but he was surprised to hear that his friend couldn't afford the kind of vacation his family took every year. Sometimes twice a year! The awkward moment caused Casey to think a lot about money. Eventually he decided to see what the Bible had to say about finances.

After asking his pastor for advice, Casey dug into the book of Proverbs. He found plenty of lessons about work and laziness, money and debt, but Proverbs 30 was the chapter that revolutionized the way Casey thought about money. Casey realized many of his payers had been about wants, not needs. Casey realized his often repeated prayer for God to bless his family was a filler and essentially meaningless. He also realized his definition of "bless" was different than Jeff's. Casey realized that for most of his adult life he had been expecting God to "bless" him with far more than needed. Casey realized he needed to change his frame of reference on the issue of money. Instead of worrying about his desired level of comfort, Casey resolved to pray that God would meet his needs.

In addition to money, Casey left Proverbs 30 with another new insight. He realized that money was only the surface level issue in Proverbs 30. The real issue was a desire to always bring glory to God's name. Casey knew he needed to spend less time praying about material things, and more time praying about sin and obedience. He needed to ask God to expose and remove sin in his life. He left his study of Proverbs committing to pray this Bible prayer in his own life.

QUESTIONS FOR DISCUSSION

1. What would it mean for you to pray that God would meet just your needs?

2. Do you really pray that God would remove the sin in your life?

3. Honestly, are you willing to pray the prayer of Agur?

CHAPTER 14

HEZEKIAH PRAYS FOR LIFE

Please, O LORD, remember how I have walked
before you in faithfulness and with a while heart,
and have done what is good in your sight. (Isaiah
38:3)

A PREVIOUS CHAPTER DETAILED THE CHARACTER OF KING
Hezekiah and one of his great prayers. When Judah was
about to be besieged by the Assyrian army, Hezekiah
prayed. Even though the prophet Isaiah had assured
the king that Jerusalem would not be overrun, Hezekiah
prayed. In response to Hezekiah's prayer, the angel of the
LORD struck down 185,000 warriors of Assyria. Hezekiah's prayer can easily be applied to situations that move
us to prayer today. And the entire story is illustrative of

Hezekiah Prays for Life

the fact that Hezekiah loved God and God blessed his reign as king (2 Kings 18:6).

Knowing this chapter of Hezekiah's life makes Isaiah 39 a tough pill to swallow. I remember reading this story for the first time, and I remember struggling to make sense of this incident. If Isaiah 39 is read in isolation, it is at best an odd story and at worst a story that makes God sound arbitrary and capricious. The story goes like this. Babylon sent a gift bearing envoy to Judah (Isaiah 39:1). The Bible records, "Hezekiah welcomed them gladly," showing them his money and weapons and commodities (Isaiah 39:2). When the grand tour was complete, Isaiah showed up. The prophet wanted to know what the Babylon envoys had been shown. When Hezekiah told Isaiah that the envoy had been shown everything, Isaiah replied that everything would one day be hauled off to Babylon. Everything included not only Hezekiah's money and weapons and commodities, but also his sons (39:5-7). The oddness continues when Hezekiah tells Isaiah that this is a "good" word from God because he knows it will happen after he's dead and gone (Isaiah 39:8).

This story makes me uneasy on several levels. First, why did God decide that all of Hezekiah's stuff and children would be exiled just because Hezekiah showed the Babylonian envoy his kingdom? This seems like an arbitrary test Hezekiah never saw coming. When read without context, it makes God sound grumpy. Second, why did God do this to Hezekiah? He was one of the few kings who did what was right before God (2 Kings 18:3). He was the king who cleansed the temple, restored worship, celebrated the Passover, and organized the priesthood (2 Chronicles 29-31). Maybe this judgment should have fallen on Hezekiah's wicked father Ahaz. But why righteous Hezekiah? Third, why did the righteous king declare God's Word of judgment on his house, his family, and his kingdom good simply because he knew it would take place after his own funeral? This seems selfish and short sighted on the part of Hezekiah.

As for the fact that Hezekiah was relieved to learn his children would face the wrath of Babylon, I can only say that Hezekiah was a sinner. He loved God. He tried to rule in a God-honoring way. But Hezekiah was a sinner. As for the fact that God's judgment was proclaimed against Judah because Hezekiah showed the Babylonian envoys everything in his kingdom, a spoonful of Biblical context brings a mountain of clarity. This context includes Hezekiah's prayer life, particularly his prayers about the Assyrian army and his own death.

Think back to the time Assyria was camped outside Jerusalem. Hezekiah was terribly afraid and he prayed that God would deliver his people so that all the nations might know that he alone was God (2 Kings 19:14-19). God delivered Hezekiah and Jerusalem by killing 185,000 Assyrian soldiers in one night (2 Kings 19:35). When other nations heard about this devastating slaughter, they decided it would be wise to get on the LORD's good side. Thus, the Bible records, "And many brought gifts to the LORD to Jerusalem and precious things to Hezekiah king of Judah, so that he was exalted in the sight of all nations from that time onward." (2 Chronicles 32:23) This is an important detail. Not only did God deliver Hezekiah from Assyria, but the spectacular slaughter of 185,000 resulted in all the nations around Judah bringing good will gifts to Hezekiah.

Hezekiah's prayer session in 2 Kings 19 (2 Chronicles 32) was powerful, but his prayer session in Isaiah 38 was personal. The Bible reveals that sometime after the Assyrian slaughter Hezekiah became sick (Isaiah 38:1). This was no head cold. This was life threatening illness. In fact, God sent Isaiah to inform Hezekiah that he needed to set his house in order because this was the end (Isaiah 38:1). There was no condition in Isaiah's message. No if-ands-or-buts. Just a simple declaration that Hezekiah was about to die.

But Hezekiah had faced death before. He knew both hopelessness and helplessness from the previous incident with Sennacherib and the Assyrian army. So Hezekiah did the only thing he knew to do. He prayed. His short prayer is recorded in Isaiah 38:2-3: "Then Hezekiah turned his face to the wall and prayed to the LORD, and said, 'Please, O LORD, remember how I have walked before you in faithfulness and with a whole heart, and have done what is good in your sight.' And Hezekiah wept bitterly."

Notice what Hezekiah did *not* pray. He did not pray that God would make him well. He did not pray that God would take away his pain. He did not pray that God would extend his life. Rather, Hezekiah prayed that God would remember. He wanted God to remember the fact that he had walked before the LORD in faithfulness with his whole heart. He wanted God to remember that he had done what was good. As he prayed this prayer, asking God to remember the overall pattern of his life, he wept bitterly.

Re-enter Isaiah. The prophet was sent back to Hezekiah to inform him that not only did God hear his prayer, and not only did God see his tears, but God had decided to add fifteen years to Hezekiah's life. The life threatening illness would not end in death, and the king would be given a new lease on life. In times of crisis, Hezekiah struggled to believe God's promises (see his uncertainty about Assyria in 2 Kings 18). In the midst of this very personal crisis, Hezekiah once again struggled to believe the promise of God. So he asked for a sign (Isaiah 38:22). This is a bold request from a dying man, but Hezekiah asked the LORD to give him a sign that he really would live fifteen more years. Surprisingly, God agreed. To assure Hezekiah that he would live another fifteen years, God caused the shadow of the sun on the dial to move backwards ten steps (Isaiah 38:8).

This brings us to the enigmatic Isaiah 39. Two miracles in Judah caught the attention of the Babylonian royal family. First, the shadow of the sun had moved back ten steps on the dial. I have no idea what this miracle involved, and apparently neither did the Babylonians. That's why they sent an envoy to Judah. 2 Chronicles 43:31 records the envoy, "had been sent to [Hezekiah] to inquire about the sign that had been done in the land." This same group was also sent to inquire about Hezekiah's health. Isaiah 39:1 records Babylon sent an envoy with "letters and a present to Hezekiah, for he heard that he had been sick and had recovered." They knew he was near death. They knew he had recovered. They wanted to know what power Hezekiah had harnessed that could both delay death and control the sun.

Make sure you have the situation clear in your mind. Hezekiah prayed for deliverance when Assyria came to fight. God delivered Hezekiah and Jerusalem by killing 185,000 Assyrian warriors. As a result of this slaughter, the surrounding nations sent tribute and treasure to Hezekiah. Later, Hezekiah found himself facing certain death. Once again he prayed for deliverance, and once again God provided deliverance in a miraculous way. As a result, the surrounding nations came to Jerusalem to inquire about the miraculous.

Isaiah 39:2 tells us that Hezekiah provided a warm welcome to his Babylonian guests. Hezekiah showed them, "his treasure house, the silver, the gold, the spices, the precious oil, his whole armory, all that was found in his storehouses." (Isaiah 39:2) This was the wealth Hezekiah

Pray Better

accumulated as a result of God slaying 185,000 Assyrian warriors, and Hezekiah gladly showed it to the Babylonian envoy. They had come to inquire about his dramatic recovery, and Hezekiah showed them all of the "stuff" with which God had blessed him. The only thing Hezekiah did not show the Babylonian envoy was God. He showed them God's blessing and provision, but he did now show them God himself. They came to learn about the power in Israel that could slay 185,000 warriors, heal the sick, and control the sun. And instead of taking these men to the temple, Hezekiah took them to his bank. Instead of telling teaching these idol worshipping pagans about the one true God, Hezekiah tried to impress them by showing off his wealth.

2 Chronicles 32:31 clarifies the situation by offering this important detail: "And so in the matter of the envoys of the princes of Babylon, who had been sent to [Hezekiah] to inquire about the sign that had been done in the land, God left him to himself, in order to test him and to know all that was in his heart." There's the explanation. The Babylonian envoys were a test. God left Hezekiah to himself to find out all that was in his heart. God answered Hezekiah's prayers for deliverance from Assyria. God answered Hezekiah's prayers for deliverance from death. Now there was only one question. As Hezekiah sat healthy and surrounded by God's blessing and provision, would Hezekiah give glory and credit and honor to the God of Israel? The answer, of course, is no. He did not give glory and credit and honor to God. He failed the test.

There are several important lessons to take away from Hezekiah's prayer in Isaiah 38. First, when you find yourself in trouble, pray. Hezekiah prayed when Assyria threatened to destroy Jerusalem, and he prayed when sickness threatened to destroy his life. When you have nowhere else to turn, turn to God in prayer. Second, when you pray, be grateful that God hears your prayers. On more than one occasion Isaiah had to reassure the fretful king that God did in fact hear his prayers (2 Kings 19:20, Isaiah 38:5). Remember, the God of heaven always hears the prayers of his people. Third, understand that prayer is powerful. 185,000 dead Assyrian warriors learned the power of prayer, and so did Hezekiah as he stared death in the face. Prayer changed both of those seemingly hopeless situations. Prayer is powerful. It's powerful because God is powerful. He controls armies and he controls sickness. Finally, when God responds to your prayers and fills your life with undeserved blessings, give God the glory and credit and honor. Do not allow yourself to be satisfied with God's gifts, and do not allow yourself to point others to God's blessings. Instead, be satisfied with God himself, and point others to the God who hears our prayers.

Learning to Pray

Matt and Katie got married right after college. They both worked good jobs close to their hometown in Kentucky. When their first kid was born, Katie stayed home. Two kids later, life was exactly where they had hoped it would be seven years earlier. Their family was healthy, and they loved their church and community. They didn't think of themselves as wealthy, but they certainly did not have to worry about money.

Then Mandy, their middle child, was diagnosed with a rare form of cancer. The doctors said they caught it early, but the prognosis was still grim. Most kids didn't survive the treatment required to combat this illness. Matt and Katie knew the road ahead would be tough. They certainly hadn't included cancer in their plan, especially one of their kids having cancer. Nevertheless, their faith was strong, and their church family was supportive.

Three years later, Mandy was cancer free. The treatment had almost been more than her young body could handle. She had spent months in the hospital. There had been trips to the emergency room and long nights. But three years later there was not a trace of cancer in Mandy's body. Matt and Katie celebrated with their medical team, their family, and their church. Those who had prayed so hard for Katie talked about the power of prayer.

Now that their daughter was healthy, Matt and Katie knew they had a new obligation they did not want to ignore. In the midst of Mandy's treatment, Matt and Katie had begun reading prayers in the Bible. They found themselves at a loss for what to pray and how to pray, so they looked to the Bible for answers. Many of the prayers they read were encouraging, but the story of King

Hezekiah was especially helpful. They read about a man who found himself in a hopeless situation and prayed. Obviously they could relate.

They also read about a man who became satisfied with God's blessings and forgot the God who gave the blessings. They knew God had given them a tremendous blessing in Mandy's health. But they wanted to make sure their family remained focused on God, even as they celebrated his blessing. As they discussed how to enjoy God's blessing while remaining focused on God himself, Matt and Katie decided to take every opportunity to tell people about God. Yes, they wanted to talk about how God answered their prayers. Yes, they wanted to be thankful and grateful for all God had done for their family. But they prayed that God would give them grace to point people to God himself instead of focusing on his blessings. They decided to start at church. Their pastor asked them to share about their experience on a Sunday. Matt and Katie emphasized the power of prayer in the face of despair. They talked about their thankfulness for answered prayer. But they pointed their church family to God, from whom all blessings flow.

QUESTIONS FOR DISCUSSION

1. Are there any seemingly hopeless situations you should begin praying about?

2. Have you been guilty of pointing people to God's blessings instead of God himself?

3. Have you failed to thank God for answering your prayers?

CHAPTER 15

JEREMIAH QUESTIONS GOD

Ah, Lord GOD! It is you who have made the heavens and the earth by your great power and by your outstretched arm! Nothing is too hard for you. (Jeremiah 32:17)

THERE ARE TIMES IN YOUR LIFE WHEN YOU REALLY WANTed to question God. Whether it's circumstance you can't understand, diagnoses you didn't want to hear, setbacks you don't want to endure, or thorns you can't seem to get rid of, there are times in your life when you really want to get some answers from God. In Jeremiah 32 we read about such a time in the life of the youthful, weeping prophet.

We are introduced to Jeremiah in Jeremiah 1:1-3. Here we learn that Jeremiah was the son of Hilkiah, a priest who lived in Anathoth in the land of Benjamin (Jeremiah 1:1). We also learn that the Word of the LORD was revealed to Jeremiah during the reigns of Josiah, Jehoiakim, and Zedekiah (Jeremiah 1:2-3). The very next verses in Jeremiah detail his specific, God-given job in life. After assuring Jeremiah that he had known him prior to forming him in his mother's womb, God commissioned Jeremiah as a prophet (Jeremiah 1:5). No application process. No aptitude test. No career path options. No guidance counselor. Just God telling this young man whose dad was a priest that he would be a prophet. And not when he grew up, but now! When he complained about his youthfulness and lack of experience, God reassured Jeremiah that his presence and power would be constant in his life (Jeremiah 1:6-10).

The timing of all this is important. Jeremiah was born in the twilight years of the Southern Kingdom of Judah. The Northern Kingdom of Israel had already been defeated and taken into exile by Assyria. Now Babylon was the dominant world power, and Judah would soon join Israel in both defeat and exile. In this setting, Jeremiah began preaching. His basic message was one of doom and gloom. He told the people that because of their sins they were about to be taken into exile in Babylon (Jeremiah 7:1-7). The false prophets in Jerusalem countered Jeremiah's message by assuring everyone that the city of David would never be overrun or defeated (Jeremiah 7:8-15). Jeremiah's job was simple. He was not called to pray for the people, because God promised not to hear any intercession for the rebels of Judah (Jeremiah 7:16-20). Instead, Jeremiah's job was simply pronouncing the certainty of destruction and exile in Judah.

As you can imagine, this message did not make Jeremiah popular in Jerusalem. In fact, most people saw him as pessimist, and even worse a traitor. He was repeatedly arrested and beaten and threatened with death, all because he obediently spoke God's Word to God's people in Jerusalem (Jeremiah 20, 26, 28).

In Jeremiah 32 we learn that King Zedekiah had thrown Jeremiah in prison because Jeremiah insisted the Babylonian army would haul the king himself into exile (Jeremiah 32:1-5). While in prison, God told Jeremiah to buy a piece of real estate from his uncle Hanamel (Jeremiah 32:6-8). Like a good prophet, Jeremiah obeyed the LORD and bought the land (Jeremiah 32:9-15). Even though Jeremiah was incarcerated, the deeds were signed, and Jeremiah asked a special favor of his assistant Baruch. Jeremiah told Baruch to stash the property deeds in a container that would last for decades because, "Houses and fields and vineyards shall again be bought in this land." (Jeremiah 32:14-15).

Understand the situation. For years Jeremiah had been telling Jerusalem that exile was coming. With Zedekiah on the throne, Jeremiah told people that exile was now imminent. While in prison, God told Jeremiah to invest in real estate in the very city that was about to be flattened by the Babylonian army. Economically, this made no sense. Jeremiah believed God's promise that, "Houses and fields and vineyards shall again be bought in this land." (Jeremiah 32:14-15) But he still had questions. So after he obeyed God, and after he stashed away his soon-to-be-worthless real estate deeds, Jeremiah prayed. Take a moment to read Jeremiah's prayer in Jeremiah 32:16-25.

What Jeremiah really wanted to ask the LORD was a one word question, "Why?" Why, with Babylon besieging the city, did God tell the prophet to dump a significant sum of money on real estate that would soon belong to Nebuchadnezzar? Eventually, Jeremiah got around to asking this question. But first he prayed a model prayer for anyone struggling with the question, "Why?" He began by acknowledging God as the all-powerful Creator (Jeremiah 32:17). He recognized the faithfulness of God (Jeremiah 32:18). He submitted to God as the Judge of all creation (Jeremiah 32:19). He trusted in God as redeemer (Jeremiah 32:20-22). He confessed the rebellion of Judah (Jeremiah 32:23). He agreed that the coming punishment was in fulfillment of God's warnings and prophecies (Jeremiah 32:23-24). Then, and only then, did Jeremiah question God. In Jeremiah 32:25 the prophet said, "Yet you, O Lord GOD, have said to me, 'Buy the field for money and get witnesses' – though the city is given into the hands of the Chaldeans." In other words, why did you make me spend money on a field that is about to belong to Nebuchadnezzar?

In the verses that follow, God reminds Jeremiah of an all-important truth he already knew. Namely, nothing is too hard for the LORD, the God of all flesh (Jeremiah 32:26-27). God also reminded Jeremiah that Jerusalem was about to be overrun because of the rampant wickedness of the people (Jeremiah 32:28-35). God explained that he had a plan to use Babylon, and he had a plan for Judah after he was done using Babylon. God promised to gather his people back (Jeremiah 32:37). He promised that once again he would be their God (Jeremiah 32:38). He promised to give the people one heart to obey (Jeremiah 32:39). He promised to make a new covenant with his people (Jeremiah 32:40). He promised to rejoice in doing them good (Jeremiah 32:41). He promised to restore their fortunes (Jeremiah 32:42-44). This was the answer to Jeremiah's question, "Why?" God wanted him to buy the land as an act of faith, showing that Jeremiah believed God's promises to one day bring the people back to the Promised Land.

In all of this, there is a tension that is not easily explained away. On the one hand, God had made many promises to bless his people. On the other hand, God had warned his people about their sin and promised punishment if they did not repent. The tension comes in when we remember that God is holy and just, while also being patient and merciful. The people of Judah clearly deserved the judgment of God to fall on their nation and their city, and we know God did not relent from this judgment. At the same time, God promised Jeremiah that one day he would forgive his people, not because of anything they would do, but simply because he was gracious and merciful. The tension is obvious. How can God punish his people and forgive his people at the same time? How can God be a holy Judge and a merciful Savior at the same time?

The answer to these questions was promised in the Old Testament and revealed in the New Testament. In the Old Testament God promised a New Covenant (Jeremiah 31:31-34, Ezekiel 36:22-36). He promised to do a work in his people that was different than anything else he had done before. This New Covenant was inaugurated by Jesus, and the tension was resolved. In the New Covenant we see God presented both as just and the justifier of the one who has faith in Christ (Romans 3:25-26). In the New Covenant we see God presented both as the Judge who punishes sin and the Savior who forgives sinners (2 Corinthians 5:21).

Ultimately Jeremiah's prayer points us forward to this New Covenant inaugurated by Jesus. More immediately, Jeremiah's prayer teaches us several important lessons about the situations in life where we find ourselves questioning God and his plan. One lesson is the fact that it is not wrong to bring our questions to God. Jeremiah questioned God, and he was not rebuked for his inquiry. Instead God gently reminded him of his character and pointed him forward to his coming salvation (Jeremiah 32:26-44). Another lesson is that our obedience must always precede our questions. God told Jeremiah to buy the field. He bought it. Then he questioned God. He didn't understand why God wanted him to buy the field, but he obeyed. The same must be true of us. Our doubts and questions must never be allowed to hinder our obedience.

A third lesson is the necessity of preaching the truth about God to ourselves. When Jeremiah questioned God's directions, he began his prayer by reminding himself of the truth about God and his power (Jeremiah 32:17). When God responded to Jeremiah's question, he began by reminding Jeremiah of the truth about himself and his power (Jeremiah 32:27). When we find ourselves questioning God, we must always preach the truth about God to ourselves. Part of this preaching involves reminding ourselves that God does in fact love his people (Jeremiah 32:18). So often, when life tempts us to question God, we begin to wonder whether or not God truly loves us. Does God really care about us? Does he really want what's best for us? The answer for Jeremiah, and the answer for us, is a resounding, "Yes!" Jeremiah looked forward, and we look back to the New Covenant inaugurated with the blood of Jesus (Matthew 26:26-29). The cross is God's declaration once and for all that no matter what our circumstances may be, he does in fact love his people (Romans 5:8). When we're tempted to question God, we must remind ourselves of the love God showed us as the cross. May our circumstances never cause us to question God's love shown at the cross of Jesus.

A final lesson about prayer is this—when we are tempted to question God and the circumstances of life, we must always remind ourselves that God does in fact have a plan. Even when we can't make sense of what God is doing in the world, God has a plan. Even when we don't understand what God is asking us to do, God has a plan. Jeremiah did not understand the reasoning behind his real estate transaction. But he obeyed, and he learned to trust in the God who has a good plan for his people (Jeremiah 1:5, 32:15, 16-44).

LEARNING TO PRAY

Brandi was the first person in her family to graduate from college. Graduation was two months away, and Brandi had much to be excited about. While many of her friends were concerned about finding a real job, Brandi had a job lined up and ready to go. A family friend used his influence to get her an interview. The firm rarely hired new graduates without experience. However, the recommendation of her dad's friend was enough to get her foot in the door. The firm not only offered her a job, but also gave her a signing bonus and agreed to pay for her moving expenses after graduation.

Brandi's mom was excited. Her daughter was about to spread her wings and step into a bright future. Brandi's dad was proud. He had worked long and hard hours to provide this opportunity for his daughter. His daughter was about to walk through doors that had never opened in his life.

Brandi was excited about her future and proud of her accomplishments, but she was also haunted. Two years earlier she attended a weekend missions conference with her church college group. The conference involved several main session speakers as well as smaller break-out sessions. In one break-out session Brandi heard about opportunities to serve for two years overseas as a student missionary. Most placements were on college campuses, and missionaries could be placed in almost any major city around the world. Brandi had always wanted to go to China, and she had always been passionate about missions. When the speaker gave the students the opportunity to sign up, Brandi took it!

Brandi applied and was accepted two months later. Her term could begin anytime over the next three years. When she first learned she had been accepted, she started looking for ways to squeeze the two year assignment into her life. She thought about putting college on hold, but her dad wasn't wild about that idea. Then she considered going on the trip after graduation. That plan was derailed by the amazing job offer. Now graduation was two months away, and Brandi didn't know what to do. Should she take the job? Should she go to China? Her compensation would allow her to give generously to missions. But she had made a commitment. She knew her parents would be disappointed. She also knew the decision could jeopardize her career opportunities.

Talking to the wife of her college pastor was a great help. Carroll told her about a time God asked Jeremiah the prophet to do something that flew in the face of common sense. Jeremiah was confused and didn't know what to do. Instead of jumping to the obvious question, "Why?" Jeremiah first prayed a prayer focused on God and his attributes and his promises. Not surprisingly, God's answer to Jeremiah was based on his attributes and his promises. Brandi knew what to do. She knew God's heart for the nations, and she knew his commands to make disciples of all nations. She knew her decision would upset some and confuse others. But after praying like Jeremiah, she began getting ready for China.

Questions for Discussion

1. What life situations have caused you to want to question God and his plan?

2. Why is it significant that Jeremiah prayed a lengthy prayer before asking God "why"?

3. Have you allowed doubts and questions to hinder your obedience to God?

CHAPTER 16

JESUS PRAYS A MODEL PRAYER

Our Father in heaven, hallowed be your name.
(Matthew 6:9)

ONE OF THE BEST KNOWN AND MOST LOVED ACCOUNTS from the life of Jesus is the Sermon on the Mount (Matthew 5-7). Matthew is the only gospel author to include this particular sermon. While Luke 7 contains teaching that is similar to Matthew's Sermon on the Mount, there are enough differences in the two passages to conclude that Matthew and Luke are describing similar but different sermons. Remember, Jesus was an itinerant preacher, and most itinerant preachers reuse the same material in different places and contexts. So while Matthew 5-7 and Luke 7 contain similar material, they are probably summaries of two different sermons.

Matthew's Sermon on the Mount contains a plethora of teaching found nowhere else in the Bible. This sermon contains the "Beatitudes" (Matthew 5:1-12). It includes Jesus telling his disciples they are the salt of the earth and the light of the world (Matthew 5:13-16). It includes Jesus declaration that he came to fulfill, not abolish, the law and the prophets (Matthew 5:17-20). It also includes Jesus challenging teaching about anger, lust, divorce, oaths, retaliation, and forgiveness (Matthew 5:21-48).

Towards the end of the Sermon on the Mount, Jesus talked about judging other people (Matthew 7:1-6). He talked about God's willingness to respond to our prayers (Matthew 7:7-11) He offered up a maxim we known today as the "Golden Rule" (Matthew 7:12-14). Jesus ended by dividing all of humanity into two groups. There are some on the narrow road and others on the wide road (Matthew 7:13-14). There are some who bear fruit and others who do not (Matthew 7:15-19). There are some who are known by Jesus and others who are not (Matthew 7:21-23). There are some who build on the rock and others who build on the sand (Matthew 7:24-27).

The teaching of Jesus recorded in this sermon defies the wisdom of this world. These words reveal the horrific depths of our depravity, and they offer the most somber of warnings. At the same time, these words provide comfort and hope to those who follow Jesus. Right in the middle of this matchless sermon, Jesus talked about spiritual disciplines. Jesus addressed the dangers of money and the importance of tithing (Matthew 6:1-4, 19-34), and Jesus addressed the importance of fasting (Matthew 6:16-18). Surely these verses contain truth needed in twenty-first century American Christianity.

These verses also contain Jesus' most direct teaching about prayer (Matthew 6:5-15). In fact, this famous sermon contains the most famous prayer in all of Christendom. Some know it as "The Lord's Prayer." Others repeat it mantra-style as "Our Father's" to go along with a prescribed number of "Hail Mary's." Many have recited it at a sporting event, wedding, funeral, or church service. The actual prayer is simple and goes like this: "Our Father in heaven, hallowed be your name. Your kingdom come, your will be done, on earth as it is in heaven. Give us this day our daily bread, and forgive us our debts, as we also have forgiven our debtors. And lead us not into temptation, but deliver us from evil." (Matthew 6:9-13)

Even as you read those ancient words, your mind was probably racing ahead, ready for the next line. These are familiar words. Certainly no one would deny the benefits of memorizing this prayer, and few would complain that so many could quote the teaching of Jesus. However, there is great irony in the popular usage of this prayer. Some churches repeat these words regularly as a mindless chant. But that's exactly what Jesus did not want his disciples to do! Other churches practically ignore the prayer, and it plays no role in the worship of the gathered church. Again, that's not what Jesus had in mind at all!

A brief look at the context will help put this prayer in perspective. Understand that prayer itself is not optional. It's mandatory. Jesus begins this section with these words, "And when you pray ..." (Matthew 6:5). That's *when* you pray. Not *if* you pray. Jesus is assuming that his people will be praying people. Add to this the fact that right before he offered up the first ever recitation of "The Lord's Prayer," Jesus said these words, "Pray then like this." (Matthew 5:9) This is not a suggestion. This is a command. Jesus is telling us we must be praying people, and he's giving us an actual prayer he wants us to pray.

Jesus does not want us to pray for an audience. He specifically warns about praying to "be seen by others." (Matthew 6:5) This warning does not preclude all corporate prayer, but it does provide a warning to those who lead corporate prayers. We must always remember that prayer is talking to God, not talking to impress other people.

Jesus wants our prayers to be simple. Prayer is a believer talking to God (Matthew 6:6). Prayer is not the accumulation of empty phrases, or mindless mantras (Matthew 6:7). Prayer does not require a minimum word count (Matthew 6:7). Prayer is not bringing new information to God (Matthew 6:8). Rather, prayer is a believer simply talking to God. Since God already knows our hearts, our prayers don't have to be lengthy or wordy. Instead, our prayers should be simple conversations with our Father.

This brings us to the prayer itself. Usually referred to as "The Lord's Prayer," it should probably be known as "The Disciples' Prayer." It is a prayer Jesus gave his disciples. It is a prayer Jesus expected his disciples to pray. It is a simple prayer, and when prayed from the heart, it is a good prayer. As you break down the six short statements, there are several important truths to remember.

When you pray, "Our Father in heaven," remember that prayer is based on a relationship. It is more like a conversation with a loving parent than a conversation with a stranger or even an acquaintance. Prayer flows out of the relationship we have with God the Father, a relationship made possible by the death and resurrection of Jesus.

When you pray, "Hallowed be your name," remember that this is the motivation of all good prayer. From Genesis to Revelation, when godly people pray, their prayers are motivated by a desire to see God's name hallowed, or made holy. Good prayer is always motivated by a desire to see God glorified in all the earth.

When you pray, "Your kingdom come, your will be done, on earth as it is in heaven," remember that prayer is more about God getting his way than us getting our way. Prayer is not a magic formula for bringing our desires to fruition. Rather, prayer involves bending our wills in submission to God's will.

When you pray, "Give us this day our daily bread," remember that God does not want us to worry about the necessities of life (Matthew 6:19-34). Rather, God wants us to be people of faith, trusting him to provide for every need. Living in a country of affluence, we must remember that this is a prayer for necessities, not luxuries.

When you pray, "Forgive our trespasses as we forgive others," remember that you are a sinner in need of constant grace. Remember that every opportunity we have to talk to the Father in prayer is a blood bought gift Jesus purchased for his people at the cross. As you pray, also remember that forgiven people are forgiving people.

When you pray, "Lead us not into temptation, but deliver us from evil," remember that, "No temptation has overtaken you that is not common to man." (1 Corinthians 10:13) Also remember that, "With the temptation he will also provide the way of escape, that you may be able to endure it." (1 Corinthians 10:13)

When you pray, not if you pray, but when you pray, pray like this.

LEARNING TO PRAY

Lacy and Rachel met at a mom's program at church. Both ladies had attended the church for years, but their paths had never crossed until recently. They discovered that their children were the same age and interested in the same things. A friendship was formed almost instantly. As the ladies spent time together, they began discussing the possibility of leading a women's Bible study in one of their homes. Lacy and Rachel were both excited about the idea, so they set up a time to discuss specifics.

At the end of their planning session, Lacy and Rachel prayed for the upcoming home Bible study. Lacy prayed first. She prayed that people would come, that God would help them know what to study and who to invite, and that God would bless the study. Then Rachel prayed, and when Rachel prayed Lacy was at a loss for words. Rachel's prayer was so different than her prayer. In fact, Rachel's prayer was different than any prayer she had ever heard before. The second Rachel said, "Amen," Lacy asked her friend where she learned to pray.

Rachel had to stop and think. Where did she learn to pray? She had never read a book on prayer. She couldn't remember ever taking a class at church about prayer. All she knew is that she grew up listening to her parents pray. These prayers were more than the obligatory pre-meal or pre-travel prayers. They were more than the vague, generic requests for God's blessing. They were more than rote recitations of formulaic prayers.

As she thought about how to answer Lacy's question, Rachel began to realize that memorizing Scripture had been a big part of how she learned to pray. She thought about the time her parents invested helping her learn the Lord's Prayer. Rachel's parents made her memorize the prayer. Later, they made her paraphrase and summarize the prayer in her own words. Eventually, Rachel began to use the framework of the Lord's Prayer as the basis for her own prayers.

Honestly, Rachel didn't even realize this was how she prayed until Lacy asked the question. But sure enough, her prayer for the upcoming ladies' Bible study was firmly rooted in the pattern of the Lord's Prayer. First she acknowledged God as God. Second, she prayed that God would be glorified in their individual lives as well as the Bible study. Third, she prayed that God's will would be done in and through their planning. Fourth, she prayed for provision and grace and obedience as she walked forward with Lacy.

Lacy left the meeting doubly excited. She was excited about the ladies' Bible study that would soon begin. She was excited about a new way to pray. Lacy began memorizing the Lord's Prayer that night. A few days later she began paraphrasing and summarizing the Lord's Prayer. Eventually she found herself using the Lord's Prayer as a framework for all of her prayers. Instead of coming to God and simply presenting a list of request, Lacy was praying like Jesus taught his disciples to pray.

QUESTIONS FOR DISCUSSION

1. Jesus assumed his people would be praying people. Would others describe you as a person of prayer? Why or why not?

2. Have you been guilty of misusing or not using this model prayer?

3. Do your prayers sound more like news reports and updates for God's benefit, or do they sound more like a simple conversation with your Father?

CHAPTER 17

JESUS PRAYS IN GETHSEMANE

*My Father, if it be possible, let this cup pass from
me; nevertheless, not as I will, but as you will.
(Matthew 26:39)*

I SUPPOSE THAT IN WRITING A BOOK ABOUT PRAYER, IT
would be impossible to ignore Jesus' prayer in Matthew
26. There is no greater prayer warrior than Jesus, and this
is the prayer Jesus prayed at the most critical moment
of his life. So this prayer must be included. However, I
include it with fear and trembling. This is most certainly
holy ground when it comes to prayer. This prayer reveals
some of the most intimate, inter-Trinitarian dialogue in
Scripture. Jesus' so called "high priestly prayer" in John 17
may be a longer, more detailed prayer. But Jesus' prayer
in Matthew 26 is filled with pathos and emotion. This is

God the Son in anguish, pouring out his heart to God the Father. This is the deep end of theology, and studying this prayer means we are wading in way over our heads.

Thirty (or so) action packed years brought Jesus to this point. Born in a barn (Luke 2:7). Welcomed into the world by angels and kings (Matthew 2:1-12, Luke 2:13-14). A contract on his infant head (Matthew 2:16-18). Taking refuge in Egypt (Matthew 2:13-15). Baptized by his cousin John (Mark 1:9-11). Tempted by Satan (Luke 4:1-13). Casting out demons (Mark 5:1-20). Healing the sick (Luke 5:12-26). Raising the dead (John 11:1-44). Preaching to multitudes (John 6:22-59). Discipling twelve men (Mark 3:13-21). You get the idea. It was an action-packed thirty years.

More recently, an eventful week brought Jesus to this critical time of prayer. On Sunday, Jesus rode into Jerusalem on a donkey (Matthew 21:1-11). Pilgrims to Jerusalem and residents of Jerusalem lined the street and welcomed Jesus as the Son of David (Matthew 21:9). On Monday, Jesus cleared the temple for the second time (Matthew 21:12-17). On Tuesday, Jesus taught in the temple, winsomely evading the theological traps of the religious establishment (Matthew 21:18-25:46). Wednesday was quiet. Thursday, Jesus celebrated the Passover with his disciples (Matthew 26:17-25). After washing the feet of his disciples, Jesus dismissed Judas to carry out the plan he had made a few days earlier (John 13:1-30). Then Jesus did the unthinkable and changed the Passover by instituting the Lord's Supper (Matthew 26:26-29). With

Judas gone and dinner complete, Jesus led his disciples to Gethsemane (Matthew 26:36).

On Friday, there would be multiple trials (Matthew 26:57-68, John 18:12-40), beatings (Matthew 27:24-31), a crucifixion (Matthew 27:32-56), and a burial (Matthew 27:57-61). On Saturday, all would be quiet as Jesus lay dead in the tomb provided by Joseph of Arimithea (Matthew 27:57). On Sunday, everything would change as Jesus was raised from the dead by the power of the Holy Spirit (Matthew 28:1-15). But before Easter Sunday, and before the cross, and before the trials, Jesus prayed. Take a minute to read Jesus' prayer in Matthew 26:36-46.

One thing this passage teaches us about prayer is the fact that prayer is hard. It is not easy. It is not for the faint of heart. It is tough. Jesus begged his disciples to stay awake with him and pray. Like so many of us, the disciples were not able to stay awake and sleep overtook them. This didn't just happen once. It actually happened three times (Matthew 26:40, 43, 45)! Here was the Son of God, in deep anguish, begging his friends to stay awake and pray. And Jesus' closest friends kept falling asleep. Was it because they didn't love Jesus? No. Was it because they thought prayer was a waste of time? No. They simply experienced what many of us have experienced. Prayer is hard. It takes work. It requires discipline. It does not come naturally to most of us.

Another thing this passage teaches us about prayer is the fact that Jesus' prayer in Gethsemane was the culmination of a life of prayer. This was not a last minute, I have nowhere else to turn, please bail me out, I really need a favor kind of prayer. Rather, prayer had been a consistent part of Jesus' life for years. At times Jesus rose early in the morning to pray (Mark 1:35). At times Jesus prayed all through the night (Luke 6:12). At times Jesus withdrew from people to pray (Luke 5:16). Jesus' life had consistently been marked by prayer, and Matthew 26 is the culmination of Jesus' prayer life.

As Jesus prayed in Gethsemane, the pathos and emotion leap off the page. This is not casual, routine prayer. One thinks of Moses, pleading with the LORD to let him enter the Promised Land (Deuteronomy 3:23). One thinks of Hannah, pouring out her heart before the LORD (1 Samuel 15). Jesus' prayer is in the tradition of these great prayers. The emotion is raw. The intensity is striking. Matthew tells us that Jesus was "sorrowful" and "troubled" (Matthew 26:38). Jesus himself told his disciples that he was "sorrowful, even to death" (Matthew 26:38). Jesus prayed with his face on the ground (Matthew 26:39). Luke adds a detail that Matthew omits, noting that as Jesus prayed he literally sweat drops of blood (Luke 22:44).

This is an odd scene. If you had been a stranger in Gethsemane, watching Jesus pray, what would you have assumed? The most logical conclusion would have been that this Jewish man was having a nervous breakdown.

While his friends napped, he was on his face, sweating blood, talking to the darkness, repeating the same prayer over and over. I don't know about you, but it reads like a nervous breakdown to me.

Now imagine you were not a stranger. Imagine you knew Jesus and had been following Jesus. Imagine you were one of the disciples and somehow you were able to stay awake to witness this intense prayer session. What would you have assumed? You had seen Jesus feed thousands with a Lunchable (John 6:1-15). You had seen Jesus walk on water and control the weather (Mark 6:45-52). You had seen Jesus stare the most crazed demoniacs in the face without blinking (Mark 5:1-20). You had seen Jesus, whip in hand, march into the temple and toss tables (John 2:13-22, Matthew 21:12-17). In all of these situations, and many more, nothing fazed Jesus! He was courageous and unshakeable in the face of storms and demons and angry mobs! Now your fearless leader is sweating blood and on his face in the darkness. What would you have assumed?

I don't know how a stranger would have interpreted these events. Nor do I know how one of Jesus' followers would have processed this scene. What I do know is the horror that drove Jesus to the edge of emotional sanity. Make no mistake, Jesus was not afraid of nails or thorns of flogging or mockery. Jesus was not afraid of being left by his closest friends. Jesus sweat blood and cried out to his Father because he understood the nature of the divine transaction that would soon take place.

Jesus knew that he would not be spared in giving himself for his people (Romans 8:31-32). Jesus knew that he who knew no sin would soon become sin (2 Corinthians 5:21). Jesus knew that he would be cursed for his people (Galatians 3:13). Jesus knew that his blood would provide the redemption price (Ephesians 1:7). Jesus knew that he would soon become the sin bearer (1 Peter 2:24). Jesus knew that the horror of Isaiah 52:13-53:12 would soon come to pass. He would be crushed for our iniquities (Isaiah 53:5). It would be the will of the LORD to crush him (Isaiah 53:10). Simply put, Jesus knew that he was about to drink the cup of the Father's wrath (Matthew 26:39, 42, 44).

And because Jesus knew these things, this was his prayer, "My Father, if it be possible, let this cup pass from me; nevertheless, not as I will, but as you will ... My Father, if this cannot pass unless I drink it, your will be done." (Matthew 26:39, 42) Theologians debate whether or not this request was even a possibility. Could God have saved the world by divine fiat? Could Jesus have skipped the cross? Could we have been saved by some other means? The answer to these questions is, no. There was no other way. Because of the reality of God's holiness and the reality of our sin, there was no other way.

Jesus knew this. As he looked forward to the horror of the cross, he did ask the Father to exhaust any other possible means of salvation. Being no other possible means, Jesus prayed, "Not as I will, but as you will ... your will be done." (Matthew 26:39, 42) This prayer has obvious application to our prayer lives. On the one hand, we ought to bring any and every request before our Father. No concern is too small. No petition too outrageous. If Jesus had the audacity to pray that the cross might not happen, we can bring all of our petitions before the Father. But on the other hand, we must always pray in alignment with the will and the character of God. We must not pray for things that violate the revealed will of the Father. We must never pray that God would do something to violate his own character. In all our requests, we must pray that God's will be done.

So Jesus prayed. He asked the Father if there were any other means of salvation. Was there any way to rescue his people without drinking the cup of the Father's wrath? Ultimately Jesus prayed that God's will and God's will alone come to pass. Then Jesus arose, woke his friends, and prepared himself to face Judas and the mob. In a matter of hours Jesus would drink the cup of the Father's wrath. He would die. He would bear our sin. He would take our punishment. There was no other way.

As we think about prayer, it is worth noting that the Bible specifically tells us that this prayer was heard. Hebrews 5:7 reveals, "In the days of his flesh, Jesus offered up prayers and supplications, with loud cries and tears, to him who was able to save him from death, and he was heard because of his reverence." Jesus prayed to the One who was able to save him from death. He was not saved from death. But he was heard because of his reverence. Reverence? How does sweating blood, laying in the dirt, and looking for a loophole translate into reverence? The answer is simple: "Not as I will, but as you will ... your will be done." (Matthew 26:39, 42) Not only was Jesus' prayer heard, but it was also answered. God's will was done. Jesus tasted death in the place of his people.

It is also worth noting that the Bible specifically tells us that Jesus tasted death on our behalf for the "joy" that was set before him (Hebrews 12:2). How does "joy" fit into the scene in Gethsemane recorded in Matthew 26? Again the answer is simple. Jesus knew that his suffering would eventually lead to his supreme glory. This is what Jesus had prayed for earlier in the night when he prayed, "Father, glorify me in your own presence with the glory that I had with you before the world existed." (John 17:5)

Jesus had humbled himself by taking the form of a servant (Philippians 2:6-7). He was about to humble himself to the point of death, even death on a cross (Philippians 2:8). As he looked forward to all that the cross would entail, Jesus submitted his life to God's will and set his eyes on the joy set before him. That joy was his glory, receiving the name above all names, and the worship of all people (Philippians 2:9-11). Thus, in the end, Jesus' prayer was a prayer that he would receive glory. As we pray, may we always pray to this end. May we always pray that Jesus receives the glory he rightfully deserves.

LEARNING TO PRAY

When he first told people he was leaving Alabama to serve overseas, Carey heard all the usual questions. People asked him about disease and danger and terrorists. Carey knew there was great risk involved in leaving Alabama for Northern Africa, but he gladly took the risk so that he could take the name of Jesus to those who had never heard the gospel.

For the most part, Carey felt very safe during his time in Northern Africa. Yes there were dangerous people and places. Yes there was risk of disease and sickness. But there were also bad parts of his home town he did not frequent. And there were plenty of people back home he tried to avoid. The same was true of his new home. Carey tried to be wise and aware, and rarely did he feel like he was in dangerous situations.

Then the unthinkable actually happened. A group of extremists raided a clinic where Carey was visiting with a fellow missionary. Several in the clinic were killed. Carey was taken hostage. His parents, Ray and Jean, knew something was wrong when they didn't hear from their son for several weeks. Finally the call came from Carey's sending agency. He had been captured, and the extremists were demanding a ransom. The extremists promised to release Carey when the ransom was paid. History told those involved that Carey would be killed no matter what.

This was the kind of situation where prayer came naturally. Ray and Jean shared the news with their church family. The pastor sent out a church wide email and even called a special Thursday night prayer service. News spread rapidly on social media, and two days later the local news ran a prime time story on Carey's abduction. Of course, Ray and Jean spent hours on their knees in prayer.

The local news, Facebook and Twitter, and the special prayer meetings had one thing in common. People were praying for Carey's safe release. To be sure, Ray and Jean prayed passionately for their son's safe release. But many people would be surprised to know that when Ray and Jean prayed for their son they did not focus on his safe release. Rather, they prayed for their son to be bold and faithful to Jesus to the end.

 Ray and Jean were retired missionaries. They knew the risks involved in missionary service, and they knew obedience to the Great Commission involved accepting risk. Jesus was the only name that could save the people of Northern Africa. Sacrifice was required to take the gospel to these people. So more than anything, Ray and

Jean prayed that God would be glorified in and through this crisis.

Ray and Jean found direction to pray in the prayers Jesus' prayed the night before he was arrested. Yes they wanted their son to be released. But ultimately they wanted God's will to be done, and they wanted God to bring glory to Jesus. If that meant Carey dying at the hands of those he tried to serve, then they would rest in the plan and the providence of God.

QUESTIONS FOR DISCUSSION

1. Why is prayer hard for most of us?

2. How do you really pray in alignment with God's revealed character and will?

3. How can we consistently pray for Jesus to be glorified?

CHAPTER 18

THE CHURCH PRAYS
FOR BOLDNESS

Grant to your servants to continue to speak your
word with all boldness. (Acts 4:29)

AFTER DYING AND BEING RAISED FROM THE DEAD, JESUS
gave his disciples very specific marching orders. As the
Father had sent Jesus into the world, Jesus was now
sending the disciples into the world (John 20:21). They
were to go and make disciples of all the nations, baptiz-
ing them and teaching them (Matthew 28:18-20). They
were to preach repentance and forgiveness of sins all
over the earth (Luke 24:47). They were to be witnesses in
Jerusalem, in Judea and Samaria, and even to the ends of
the earth (Acts 1:8).

The book of Acts recounts how the disciples embarked on
this mission. After the Holy Spirit arrived on the day of

Pentecost, it was Peter who stood up to preach the first Christian sermon (Acts 2:1-36). Peter used several Old Testament passages as he confronted sin and pointed his audience to Jesus. At the end of his message, Luke tells us that 3,000 people were baptized and added to the church (Acts 2:41). The very next verse explains that this overnight mega-church was "devoted" to four simple things: the teaching of the apostles, fellowship, breaking bread, and prayer (Acts 2:42). Each of these were important, but prayer in particular was about to play a central role in the life of this infant church.

Acts 3 recounts how Peter healed a lame man as he and John made their way to the temple during the hour of prayer (Acts 3:1-10). This miracle attracted a crowd, and Peter took the opportunity to preach another sermon. Again Peter referred to the Old Testament, confronted sin, and pointed his audience to Jesus (Acts 3:11-26).

As Peter preached, he and the other apostles were confronted by some of the religious establishment in Jerusalem. Luke notes these men were "annoyed" that the apostles were still talking about the resurrection of Jesus (Acts 4:2). To deal with this problem, the religious establishment in Jerusalem had Peter and John arrested. This was truly a case of too-little-too-late. By this time, the Jesus movement had grown to 5,000 men (Acts 4:4).

The next day Peter and John, still in custody, were brought before the high priestly family (Acts 4:5-6). Understand that this was Annas and Caiaphas and the rest of the men who had led in the arrest, trial, and crucifixion of Jesus. These were men with blood on their hands. Men who were not afraid to deal with "problems" in the most severe ways.

Peter was undeterred. Filled with the Holy Spirit, Peter looked these wicked men in the face and did what he had been doing a lot of lately, he preached. Once again Peter exposed sin and pointed his audience to Jesus, this time insisting that there was "no other name under heaven given among men by which we must be saved." (Acts 4:12) Upon hearing this, the religious establishment found themselves between a rock and a hard place. On the one hand, they noted the boldness of Peter and John (Acts 4:13). On the other hand, they feared that many more in Jerusalem would come to believe Peter's message about Jesus (Acts 4:18). In the end, they resorted to bully tactics. These religious leaders charged Peter and John to shut up (Acts 4:19). Peter explained that he and John would not be able to be quiet about Jesus, and the religious leaders responded with more threats (Acts 4:19-21). It does not take a literary genius to read between the lines here. These were the men who had just arrested, tried, and lobbied for the murder of Jesus. Now they were threatening to do the exact same thing to Peter and John.

In the end, Peter and John were released, and at this point the story takes a very non-American turn. If this story were being written about believers in modern day

America, the recently threatened believers would probably go directly to the nearest law firm without "passing go." They would explain how they had been mistreated, and arrested, and threatened. They would take their stand on the religious freedoms afforded them by the Constitution. They would look for a legal or political remedy to this horrific situation. They might even seek the assistance of a sympathetic congressman or senator.

But that's not how the story of Acts 4 developed. Instead of seeking a legal or political remedy that would allow them greater freedom, Peter and John went to church. Luke tells us that, "When they were released, they went to their friends and reported what the chief priests and the elders had said to them." (Acts 4:23) Surely Peter did most of the story telling, and as soon as he finished the entire church broke out into a spontaneous prayer meeting. Luke writes, "They lifted their voices together to God." (Acts 4:24). Take a moment and read their prayer as Luke records it in Acts 4:24-31.

The first noteworthy aspect of this prayer was the fact that it was a corporate prayer. This was not a group of individuals praying for the same thing. This was a church praying together for the same thing. Their voices were lifted together, as one (Acts 4:24). This is a missing emphasis in many churches. We all agree about the power and importance of prayer, but our worship services and our church schedules reveal the sad fact that our highest priority is not corporate prayer. In modern day America, our highest priorities (even in the church) are probably entertainment and busyness. We want to enjoy ourselves, and we want to get something accomplished. We hardly have time for prayer, much less corporate prayer where someone might pray past the allotted time.

Please don't hear this as a complaint about the decline of Wednesday night prayer meetings. I am not suggesting that the Wednesday night prayer meeting needs to be revived, nor am I suggesting that praying together at fixed intervals and for a certain duration will cure all that ills our churches. I am simply saying there is something special about corporate prayer. There is something powerful and unifying about a church praying together. It really doesn't matter when and where that happens, but it certainly needs to happen.

The second noteworthy aspect of this corporate prayer is the fact that good theology formed the foundation of their prayers. The first thing they prayed was a declaration of God's sovereignty (Acts 4:24). They expressed their belief that God was sovereign over creation (Acts 4:24). They expressed their belief that God was sovereign over revelation (Acts 4:25-26). They expressed their belief that God was sovereign over salvation (Acts 4:27-28). Before they ever made a request of God, they affirmed their belief in his sovereignty. They knew they weren't telling God something he didn't already know. Rather, they were reminding themselves of something we easily forget. God is sovereign over all things. Our prayers are not news updates, nor are they course adjustments. In prayer we are talking to the God who is totally and completely sovereign over all things.

This high view of God didn't discourage their prayers, but it did shape their prayers. It did not make them fatalists resigned to accept whatever may come, but it did shape the requests they made of God. The first request is found in Acts 4:29. The church simply asked God to look on the threats that had been made against them. Isn't that strange? When I think about many of the prayer meetings I've sat through, I don't remember many people asking God to simply "look" on a bad situation. I remember people asking God to heal another person. I remember people asking God to keep someone safe. I remember people asking God to right wrongs and make things easier for us to serve him. But these believers didn't ask for any of those things. They just asked God to "look" on the threats.

Their theology drove this request. They were aware that God knew everything that was going on. They understood that God was not wringing his hands trying to think of an appropriate response. They believed with all their heart that God was totally and completely sovereign. So they simply asked God to "look" on their situation. This is another way of praying what Jesus prayed in Gethsemane, "your will be done" (Matthew 26:39, 42). They wanted God to do what he thought was best in the situation. If that meant providing safety, so be it. If that meant facing great danger, so be it.

The second request followed quickly after the first. The church asked God to grant them boldness to continue speaking the truth about Jesus (Acts 4:29). The following verse shows us that this church recognized God as the great actor in this drama (Acts 4:30). Yes, they had just stood bold before the same religious leaders who had Jesus murdered, but they knew that left to themselves they were powerless. So they prayed for boldness. Luke tells us that when they had prayed the place was shaken, the Spirit filled the church, and their prayer for boldness was answered (Acts 4:31).

Two final lessons are worth pointing out. First, we should pray for things we know God desires. Put another way, we should pray for things God has already commanded. This seems counterintuitive to the pragmatic American mind. We wonder, "If God wants such-and-such to come about, and if God is really sovereign, won't it happen even if we don't pray?" The church in Acts didn't waste time thinking about such foolish questions. They just prayed, and they prayed for the things they knew God wanted. They knew Jesus had sent them out to be witnesses (Acts 1:8). They prayed that God would make them bold witnesses. And God was happy to answer this prayer (Acts 4:31). Today our churches should pray for things we know God desires. We should pray for boldness. We should pray for new disciples among the nations. We should pray for obedience and holiness in the church. We should pray for faith and courage in the face of increasing political and cultural opposition. We should pray fervently for the things God wants.

Second, our prayers are only as good as our theology. If our view of God falls in line with the message espoused by the health and wealth preachers, our prayers will not be God-honoring prayers. If our view of God falls in line with the message of the open theist theologians, our prayers will not be God-honoring prayers. If our view of God falls in line with the lets-be-cool-and-relevant-and-talk-about-Jesus-like-he's-just-one-of-your-buddies preachers, our prayers will not be God-honoring prayers.

We must see God as sovereign over all things, creation, revelation, and even salvation. We must believe in a God who knows all things and can do all things. We must believe in a God who has a definite and fixed plan for history. And when we believe the truth about God, our prayers will start to sound more like the prayer of Acts 4. We will pray for what God wants. We will pray in response to God's revealed will. And we will pray together.

LEARNING TO PRAY

Pam and Steve never dreamed that getting married would be good for business, but it was. Pam baked cakes and Steve was a wedding photographer. Both were good at their respective jobs, and the convenience of hiring a baker and photographer at the same time only helped their businesses grow. Most weeks they turned down multiple weddings because their schedule was booked solid.

Last September Pam and Steve were contacted about a wedding for a gay couple. The couple wanted Pam to provide the cake and Steve to take the pictures. They were flexible about their dates because the wedding was over a year away. Pam and Steve had talked about this exact situation. They knew small businesses had been fined in Montana and New Mexico for refusing to provide services at gay weddings. Months earlier they had actually prayed together, asking God for wisdom and compassion and conviction. They knew where they stood on the issue, and their decision had been made before the request was received.

Pam and Steve initially told the couple they were too busy to accept the job. When the couple offered to change the date several times, Steve finally explained that he and his wife had religious and moral objections to gay marriage. Steve tried to explain that participating in the ceremony would violate their strongly held religious convictions.

Less than a month later Pam and Steve received two certified letters in the mail. These letters notified them that refusing to provide services for the wedding in question put their respective businesses in violation of the city's "Fair Business Ordinance." This ordinance prohibited for-profit business from refusing service to anyone because of sexual orientation. Pam and Steve would each have to pay a significant fine or perform the services. Even if they paid this fine, Pam and Steve knew they couldn't afford to pay many more in the future.

The next day, Pam and Steve asked their small group to pray about their dilemma. Initially the group was outraged. Several made comments about the "fairness" of the Fair Business Ordinance. Others wanted to start a petition, possibly to recall elected local officials, possibly to revoke the ordinance. Steve admitted that he was frustrated with the situation. He knew that if he had simply told the couple he was too busy to perform services, he wouldn't be in this mess. Ironically, it was his honesty that put his back against the wall.

After admitting his frustration, Steve encouraged the group to resist the temptation to be angry. He also pointed them to Acts 4 where the church prayed for boldness in the face of persecution. Steve knew his situation was far different than the early church. His life was certainly not at stake in this issue, but his livelihood most certainly was. While he didn't want to be cruel to anyone, he did not want to back down from his convictions. Steve asked the group to remember the sovereignty of God as they prayed, and he asked the group to pray that God would give Pam and him courage to do what was right.

Questions for Discussion

1. What does corporate prayer look like in your church? What should it look like?

2. Do your prayers sound like you are talking to the supremely sovereign God?

3. Do you ever pray specifically for something you know God wants?

CHAPTER 19

PAUL PRAYS FOR THE CHURCH IN EPHESUS

To him who is able to do far more abundantly
than all that we ask or think. (Ephesians 3:20)

THE APOSTLE PAUL WAS A PRAYER WARRIOR, ESPECIALLY
when it came to praying for churches (Romans 1:8-10, 1
Corinthians 1:4-9, Galatians 6:18, Ephesians 1:15-23, 3:14-
21, Philippians 1:1-11, Colossians 1:3-14, 1 Thessalonians
1:2-3, 2 Thessalonians 1:3-12). Paul prayed for churches he
planted and churches other people planted. Paul prayed
for healthy churches and dysfunctional churches. Pal
prayed for holiness in the church. Paul prayed for leaders
in the church. Paul gave thanks for good churches and
prayed for repentance in unhealthy churches.

All of the prayers listed above can teach us how to pray for
our churches today. Nevertheless, Paul's prayers for the

190

church in Ephesus are truly remarkable. These prayers are among the most moving and beautiful prayers in all the Bible. These prayers are marked by high theology and striking prose. These prayers are not the prayers of an amateur. These prayers are the prayers of a man who has spent countless hours on his knees interceding for churches.

There is an important lesson about prayer here. Previous chapters highlighted the fact that prayer does not have to be fancy or flowery. There is undoubtedly nothing wrong with simple, ordinary prayers. Jesus even warned about praying fancy prayers and long prayers just to be heard by others (Matthew 6:5-8). While all of this is true, we must admit that there is nothing inherently evil about complex, flowery, theological prayers. Yes, God hears the simplest cries of our hearts, but does that mean we should only pray simple prayers? Surely not. After all, the book of Psalms contains many prayers that are written in flowery, beautiful, and moving language. Add to Psalms the prayers Paul prayed for the church in Ephesus. These prayers are stunning in their depth.

Take a moment to read Paul's prayers for the church in Ephesus. You will find them in Ephesians 1:15-23 and 3:14-21. When you've read them, read them again. When you've read them twice, read them in the context of the entire book of Ephesians and Acts 19. Reading all of Ephesians and one chapter of Acts will only take you a few minutes, and reading these passages will be more fruitful for you than reading anything I have to say. When you've done all that, read Paul's prayers one more time. Soak up the deep doctrine. Feel the emotion pouring out of Paul as he prays for the church he started in Ephesus.

In Paul's first prayer (Ephesians 1:15-23) there are several things to note. First, Paul celebrated the church in Ephesus because they bore the two essential marks of a church. The church in Ephesus had faith in Jesus and love for each other (Ephesians 1:15). Because these things were true in Ephesus, Paul said, "I do not cease to give thanks for you, remembering you in my prayers." (Ephesians 1:16)

As you pray for your church, keep these verses in mind. As you pray for churches in your community, keep these verses in mind. As you pray for church leaders, keep these verses in mind. There are so many things "not right" in our churches, and there are so many things that we could do better. But if these two marks are present in a church, we should give thanks. Does a church have faith in Jesus? Does a church love other people? If these things are true, we can rejoice and give thanks. Does that mean we then sit back and stop praying for positive change in our churches? Absolutely not! It does mean that when we pray for positive change in our churches, we must remember to give thanks where thanks is due. Be thankful for a church that trusts Jesus and loves people.

Second, Paul's first prayer is marked by a deep desire that the believers in Ephesus would grow in their faith and knowledge of God. Paul uses words like "wisdom" and "revelation" and "knowledge" and "enlightened" and "know" (Ephesians 1:17-23). He does not want them to remain infants in Christ. Rather, he wants them to grow in their understanding of who Jesus is and what he had accomplished on their behalf.

This desire for growth is missing in many churches today. We want to be entertained and we want to experience something exciting. But how many of us want to put in the time and effort to grow deep roots in our understanding of God? How many of us can genuinely say we want to understand salvation better next week than we do this week? How many of us can say we are fervently praying for a greater knowledge of God and his Word? We are enamored with numbers and decisions when we should be praying for disciples who know all that Jesus commanded us (Matthew 28:18-20). We do a decent job of praying for the health of people who are sick and the safety of people who are traveling. But we need to spend more time praying that our churches would be obsessed with sound doctrine.

Finally, in Paul's first prayer he directs the believers in Ephesus to gaze on the beauty of their King. In Ephesians 1:20-23 Paul moves from the resurrection to the ascension to the exaltation of Jesus. This exalted Jesus rules over the entire cosmos, and especially over the church (Ephesians

1:22-23). How many of our issues and problems in church would simply disappear if we remained focused on Jesus as the sovereign Lord over all creation and head of the church? Paul understood the importance of seeing Jesus as King, so he prayed that the church in Ephesus would always acknowledge the Lordship of Jesus.

Paul's second prayer is found in Ephesians 3:14-21. It seems that Paul intended to start his prayer in Ephesians 3:1 (notice the phrase "For this reason" in Ephesians 3:1 and 14). However, before he actually prayed, Paul stopped to talk about what God has done to save sinners (Ephesians 3:1-13). This is the same pattern of Ephesians 1:2-23. First, God acts to save sinners. Second, God tells sinners what he has done on their behalf. Then, and only then, do saved sinners respond in worship and prayer.

Notice that when Paul prays in Ephesians 3, not only does he pray for the Ephesians, and not only does he pray in light of God's glorious salvation. He also prays on his knees (Ephesians 3:14). Some may argue that "I bow my knees" is Paul's way of saying "I'm praying for you." But I think there's more to it than that. I believe Paul really is on his knees praying for the church in Ephesus. I believe Paul understood that our physical posture before God is often a picture of our heart. And as Paul prayed for his friends in Ephesus, he literally humbled himself before the Father and bowed low before God. The condition of Paul's heart is also revealed in the fact that before Paul asked God to do anything for the Ephesians, he stopped to acknowledge God as God. Paul confessed that God was the Creator of all people (Ephesians 3:15). In his posture and in his prayer, Paul is putting himself in his place, and he's putting God in God's place.

With everyone in their proper place, Paul makes two simple requests on behalf of the church. First, Paul prays that God would strengthen them spiritually (Ephesians 3:16-17). Second, Paul prays that these believers would know the love of God that surpasses knowledge (Ephesians 3:17-19). This is obviously an impossible request. How can someone know something that surpasses knowledge? How can someone comprehend the dimensions of God's love? How can a finite group of people be filled with the fullness of the infinite God? It can only happen when we pray to the God who, "is able to do far more abundantly than all that we ask or think." (Ephesians 3:20). So Paul prayed to this God, asking him to do the impossible so that Jesus might receive glory from the church forever and ever (Ephesians 3:21).

These are remarkable prayers. And it's worth asking ourselves, "Do we pray like this for our church? Do we pray like this for other believers?" We pray for sickness and health concerns, and surely these were very real in Ephesus. We pray for safety and comfort, and surely these were needed in Ephesus. We generically seek God's blessing for our lives and our families and our churches, and surely the Ephesians wanted to be blessed by God. Then there's Paul, and if I'm honest I have to admit that his prayers are different than mine. Paul did not pray general, vague prayers. Paul did not pray for so many of the things that dominate our prayer meetings. Instead, Paul specifically prayed that this church would grow deep roots in Jesus, knowing and understanding and growing in sound doctrine. He prayed that they would "know" the truth about Jesus their King.

And when Paul had prayed for the church in Ephesus, he turned the tables and implored them to pray. In Ephesians 5:15-21, Paul urged the Ephesians to pray as an act of worship. Then in Ephesians 6:10-20, Paul urged the Ephesians to pray as an act of war. May we follow Paul's example in prayer, and may we take up this charge to pray. I hope you don't take the sick folks off your prayer list, and I hope you keep praying for people when they travel. But I also hope your prayers are an act of true worship, acknowledging God. I hope your prayers are an act of war, praying for the evangelist and his audience. I hope you pray for your church to grow deep roots in the truth about Jesus.

LEARNING TO PRAY

William attends the men's prayer meeting every Friday morning at his church. Occasionally there is a guest speaker of some kind, but most Fridays are extremely predictable. First the men gather in the back of the worship center for corporate prayer. Then they break into small groups for personal prayer. Finally they go down the hall for breakfast. Sometimes William wonders how many men are there only for breakfast, but then he tells himself it's just good to have a crowd at 6:00 AM on a Friday morning.

In addition to the predictable Friday morning routine, William is occasionally troubled by the predictable prayer requests. Usually the first to speak up are those who have a sick relative or friend. What bothers him most is that most of the guys don't just ask for prayer for the sick. Instead, they tell long dramatic stories that feel like attempts to conjure up sympathy. To make things worse, as more health related requests are shared, each dramatic story feels like an attempt to upstage the previous tragedy. After several of these requests are shared with the large group, someone usually jumps in and asks for prayer for the United States. Again, these requests feel less like appeals for prayer and more like complaints about politicians and their progressive agendas.

The requests shared in small groups are rarely different than those shared with the entire group. In fact, most of the time William's group just talks about the drama discussed during the larger prayer time. When they finally move past these crisis situations, the men in William's group have a tendency to focus on their kids. As his friends request prayer for their kids, William notices that most of these men only pray about problems their kids are having. Marriage problems. Money problems. School problems. Health problems.

The real struggle for William involves something he's been studying for the past few months. As he vented his frustrations to his wife, she suggested that William read through the New Testament to see what kinds of things the early church actually prayed for. In reading, William was shocked to find so few people praying that God would change their circumstances. William was also shocked by the way Paul prayed for the churches he left behind. Paul didn't pray that God would fix all of the problems people faced, and he rarely prayed for those who were ill. Instead, Paul's prayers seemed to be centered on an unshakable desire for people and churches to know Jesus.

This discovery has revolutionized the way William prayed. It's also revolutionized the way he approaches prayer meeting. On Friday mornings, he still prays for those who are sick, and he still prays for his friends and their families and their problems. However, in praying for those who are sick or facing crises, William focuses on praying that these people would know God even in the midst of pain and suffering. He prays this for his family, for his church, and even for himself. William's prayers become consumed with a desire for people to know Jesus regardless of their circumstances.

QUESTIONS FOR DISCUSSION

1. Are you growing in your ability to pray? Are you moving beyond simple prayers to prayers that con-

tain deep theological truth? Are you growing in your knowledge of doctrine?

2. Do your prayers reflect and acknowledge the salvation secured by Jesus?

3. What requests dominate your prayer life? Health? Safety? Or spiritual growth?

CHAPTER 20

JOHN PRAYS A FINAL PRAYER

*Amen. Come, Lord Jesus! The grace of the Lord
Jesus be with all. Amen. (Revelation 22:20-21)*

IT'S FITTING THAT THE BIBLE ENDS WITH A PRAYER AND
an amen. The book of Revelation is an unveiling of truth
God gave the apostle John. And when that unveiling
was complete, John responded to God's revelation with
prayer. This is the essence of prayer. It has always and
must always be this way. God speaks, then we respond in
prayer. And until God speaks, we have nothing meaning-
ful to say. So it is right that the Bible ends with prayer.
It is fitting that the story of God's relationship with
humanity, a story that has been supernaturally revealed
to us, ends with one of us responding in prayer.

John's prayer is a simple one. After Jesus assures John that he will be coming soon, John simply writes, "Amen. Come, Lord Jesus! The grace of the Lord Jesus be with all. Amen." (Revelation 22:20-21) Note that John is praying for something Jesus just promised would happen, and happen soon. Jesus said he was coming soon. John prayed that Jesus would come. Throughout the Bible, the best prayer warriors made a habit of praying for things that God had already promised to do. I realize this seems redundant to the American mind. We wonder why we should ask God to do something he's already promised to do. I know that in my better moments I view this practice as strange, and in my worse moments I see this practice as a waste of time. I mean seriously, if God promised to do something he's not going to be frustrated by my lack of asking him to do it, right? At this point, I have to stop and remind myself that time and time again, the best prayer warriors prayed for things God had already promised. So instead of wondering whether or not my prayers are a waste of time, I should stop wasting time with foolish questions and pray.

John prayed. He prayed that Jesus would do what he had promised to do. He prayed that Jesus would "come." (Revelation 22:20) To understand what John meant by this prayer, one has to go back and review the book of Revelation. When John prays that Jesus would come, he's praying that the Jesus of Revelation 1 would come. This is the Jesus whose eyes are like flaming fire and who has a sharp two-edged sword coming out of his mouth (Revelation 1:12-16). This is the Jesus who's mere presence caused John to fall down as if he were dead (Revelation 1:17). Think about that! The last time John saw Jesus he fell on his face like a dead man, and now John is praying that Jesus would come! This is not Jesus your "buddy" or "pal." This is not Jesus who gives you a high five and acts like one of the guys. This is the supreme, sovereign Lord of all, and John wants him to come.

There's more. When John prays that Jesus would come, he's praying that the Jesus of Revelation 2-3 would come. This is the Jesus who holds the churches in the palm of his hand, and who threatens the worst if his people refuse to repent. This is the same Jesus who receives the worship of heaven and earth and all of creation in Revelation 4-7, and who pours out his wrath on those who dwell on the earth in Revelation 6-18.

When John prays that Jesus would come, he's praying that the Jesus of Revelation 19-22 would come. This is the Jesus who comes both as a bridegroom for his bride (Revelation 19:7) and the King who will rule all kings (Revelation 19:11-16). This is the Jesus who will rule during the millennium (Revelation 20:1-6), vanquish Satan into the lake of fire (Revelation 20:7-10), and judge the living and the dead (Revelation 20:11-15). This is the Jesus who will usher in the new heavens and the new earth, and who will bring his people safely into the New Jerusalem (Revelation 21). This is the Jesus who will offer his people access to the river of life and the tree of life (Revelation

22). And in praying for Jesus to come, John is telling Jesus that he is ready for all of these things to happen. He's ready for Jesus to judge the world. He's ready for Jesus to vindicate his people. He's ready for all of creation to bow before the King.

All of this flows from the book of Revelation, but John also has a bigger vision in mind when he prays that Jesus would come. John's prayer doesn't just come at the end of Revelation, it also comes at the end of the Bible. So when John prays that Jesus would come, he's basically praying that all of the unfulfilled promises of God would come to fruition. John is praying that the son of the woman would finally crush the head of the serpent (Genesis 3:15). John is praying that God's promises to Abraham would finally be fulfilled, promises for land and descendants as numerous as the stars in the sky (Genesis 12:1-3, 15:1-6, 17:1-8). John is praying that God's promise to David would finally be realized, a promise that one of David's descendants would sit on the throne forever (2 Samuel 7:13-16). John is praying that God's promises through Isaiah would come to pass, promises that salvation would come to pass for God's people and that judgment would come to pass for God's enemies (Isaiah 62-66). John is praying that God's promise through Daniel would come to pass, a promise that the Son of Man would receive dominion and glory and a kingdom (Daniel 7:13-14). John is praying that all these promises would be realized in the return of Jesus, and that every knee would bow and every tongue confess that Jesus Christ is Lord (Philippians 2:10-11).

Clearly this is a prayer we should pray. Verbatim. Word for word. We should pray it as simply as John prayed it. When we are discouraged by the wickedness of this world, and when we are desperately clinging to the promises of God, we should pray that Jesus would come. We should also allow the spirit of this prayer to shape all of our praying. Whether we are praying for the infirm or those traveling, for churches or for missionaries, for personal struggles or people in positions of leadership, we must always pray that Jesus would receive the glory and honor he rightfully deserves. To that end, we pray with John, "Amen. Come Lord Jesus!"

LEARNING TO PRAY

Derek is in a funk. After months of trying to put his finger on the problem, Derek thinks he's beginning to diagnose his malaise. Maybe it's the newspaper he reads each morning. From front to back the stories focus on political partisanship, high level scandals, crime, and natural disasters. Maybe it's the social media he monitors throughout the day. Facebook, Twitter, it's all the same. Endless pages of gossip, selfies, drama, whining, and drivel. Maybe it's the evening news. The local stations and the cable stations offer different talking heads, but their subject matter is largely the same. These programs are dominated by arguments, division, and hate.

At one point Derek hoped political change would bring about a new reality. That hoped faded quickly. Then

Derek hoped an improved economy would bring about a new reality. Again, that hoped faded quickly. Several times Derek has fallen into the trap of thinking a change in his personal life would bring about a new reality. He prayed that graduation would come quickly. He prayed that a job would come quickly. He prayed that a wife would come quickly. He prayed that children would come quickly. All of those things came in God's time, and none of them brought about the peace Derek was looking for. Now Derek is praying that his children would grow up quickly!

Last week his pastor concluded a sermon series through the book of Revelation. While the apocalyptic imagery and end times theories made his head spin at times, the pastor's concluding sermon rang through loud and clear. Although it wasn't one of the pastor's main points, Derek realized mid-sermon that the peace he had been looking for and the peace he had been praying for would never fully come until Jesus returned. For the first time Derek empathized with the last prayer of the Bible, "Amen. Come Lord Jesus!"

This realization led to a change in Derek's prayer life. He still prayed for his country and his family and his personal needs. But he stopped putting his hope in better circumstances and started putting his hope on the second coming of Christ. Regularly he found himself echoing the prayer of Revelation 22, "Amen. Come Lord Jesus!"

QUESTIONS FOR DISCUSSION

1. As you pray, are you listening to God's revelation in Scripture before speaking?

2. Do you make a habit of praying for things God has already promised to do?

3. Do your prayers reveal a desire for God's unfulfilled promises to be fulfilled?

Conclusion

My prayer is that the prayers of God's Book would shape the way we pray. I pray these prayers would make us think about the things we spend so much time praying about, as well as the things we rarely pray about. I pray these prayers would make us think about the emotion that is either present or absent in our prayers. I pray these prayers would cause us to redouble our efforts in learning sound doctrine and good theology. I pray these prayers have been a mirror exposing the apathy of our prayer lives, and I pray these prayers will be an encouragement driving us to our knees in prayer. I pray that these prayers would force us to examine our personal prayer lives as well as our corporate prayer lives. Most of all, I pray that we would pray. These twenty prayers paint a picture of very different people praying for very different things in very different circumstances. But all of them prayed. They prayed to the God of Abraham and Isaac and Jacob. They prayed that God would receive the glory he deserves. They prayed that God would keep his promises to his people. May we pray the same way.